Date Due

	OCT 2 7 2000		

Other business books
from *Inc.* magazine:

301 Great Management Ideas
Edited by Sara P. Noble,
Introduction by Tom Peters

Anatomy of a Start-Up:
27 Real-Life Case Studies
Why Some New Businesses
Succeed And Others Fail
Edited by Elizabeth K. Longsworth

How to *Really* Create a Successful
Marketing Plan
By David E. Gumpert

How to *Really* Start Your Own Business
By David E. Gumpert

How to *Really* Create a Successful
Business Plan
By David E. Gumpert

MANAGING PEOPLE

PROVEN IDEAS

FOR MAKING YOU & YOUR PEOPLE
MORE PRODUCTIVE

MANAGING PEOPLE

PROVEN IDEAS

FOR MAKING YOU & YOUR PEOPLE MORE PRODUCTIVE

From America's

SMARTEST SMALL COMPANIES

EDITED BY SARA P. NOBLE

Managing People
101 Proven Ideas
For Making You
& Your People More Productive

Designer: Robert Lesser

Portions of this book were originally
published in *Inc.* magazine.

This publication is designed to provide
accurate and authoritative information in
regard to the subject matter covered. It is sold
with the understanding that the publisher is
not engaged in rendering legal, accounting, or
other professional service. If legal advice or
other expert assistance is required, the services
of a competent professional person should
be sought.

Library of Congress Catalog Card Number:
91-078407

ISBN 1-880394-02-2 (Paperback)
ISBN 1-880394-04-9 (Hardcover)

First Edition

A
C
K
N
O
W
L
E
D
G
E
M
E
N
T
S

One of the most rewarding aspects of managing people is being able to recognize and heap praise on those who have done fine work. As the editor of this book on managing people, I would like to do just that for the writers and editors of *Inc.* magazine. If not for them, this book would not be possible. Most of the 101 ideas come directly from the pages of *Inc.* and represent the hard work, good business instincts, and incisive reporting skills that each member of *Inc.* is known for.

One person deserving special mention is Ellyn Spragins, who currently writes the "Managing People" section of the magazine. A good many items in this book are hers. Other well-represented contributors in these pages are Jill Andresky Fraser, Susan Greco and Teri Lammers. In addition, recognition goes to all the other writers and editors presently at *Inc.* who have had any part in these ideas over the years, including Alessandra Bianchi, Leslie Brokaw, Bo Burlingham, John Case, Michael Cronin, Susan Freeman, Michael Hopkins, Nancy Lyons, Robert Mamis, Martha Mangelsdorf, Anne Murphy and Bruce Posner. And most particularly, my thanks go to Jeff Seglin, Senior Editor at *Inc.*, who is a constant source of editorial assistance.

Recognition also goes to George Gendron, Editor-in-Chief and Bo Burlingham, former Executive Editor, both of whom conducted the interviews that are reprinted here. The quality of these interviews, as judged by the openness and enthusiasm exhibited by the CEOs, is due in large part to the extraordinary skills and perspicacity of these two editors.

Specific to the book itself, I'd like to thank Robert Lesser—for his fine book design and "cool" under pressure, Ed Coleman—for saving me untold time with his flawless inputting, and Susan Kron—for her last-minute read of loose ends and loose lines. At *Inc.* Subsidiary Publishing, thanks go to Hilary Glazer and Jan Spiro for all their attentive support.

Sara P. Noble, Editor
Scituate, Mass., May 1992

101 MANAGING PEOPLE IDEAS

FOREWORD...PAGE I

HIRING
1-15

Inexpensive recruiting techniques...
Writing ads for better response...Conducting
effective interviews...Employee leasing...Hiring
tests...Prospecting new hiring sources...

TRAINING
16-23

Orientation methods...Improving employees'
service to customers...Cross-training...Sales
training programs...Overcoming illiteracy...

MOTIVATION
24-33

Spicing up boring jobs...Making teams
work...Improving the office
environment...Imaginative events...

COMMUNICATIONS
34-45

Keeping staff informed...Encouraging
suggestions...Sharing the numbers...Managing
at-home staff...Grievance procedures...CEO
contact...Building employee confidence...

PRODUCTIVITY
46-54

Improving work scheduling...Productivity
incentive programs...Running effective and
short meetings...Drug programs...Safety
enforcement...Time-management techniques...

INCENTIVES
55-61

Low-cost but meaningful
rewards...Recognition programs...Timing of
rewards...Incentivizing staff to reduce costs,
increase sales, and improve collections...

SALARY & BONUSES
62-68

Alternatives to year-end bonuses...Rethinking
quotas and commissions...International
compensation...Merit increases...

LONG-TERM COMPENSATION
69-76

Profit-sharing plans that motivate...
Successful 401(k)s...Hassle-free long-term
programs...ESOPs...Phantom stock...

BENEFITS
77-84

Manageable cafeteria plans...Employee-assis-
tance and wellness programs...Making
employee-insurance contributions less
painful...Reining in workers' comp costs...

PERFORMANCE REVIEWS
85-90

Peer appraisals...Salary review
systems...Benchmarking performance...
Action-oriented reviews...

FIRING
91-96

Options for avoiding layoffs...Dealing
with bad attitudes...Last-chance
techniques...Guarding against employee
lawsuits...

LAW
97-101

Overtime pay violations...Effective
non-compete agreements...Sexual harassment
policies...Using independent contractors...

C O N T E N T S

KEN IVERSON  CEO OF NUCOR CORP.

The "father of the minimill" manages Nucor according to one principle:
Simplicity—simplicity in organization, compensation, and strategy.

PAGE 129

JACK STACK  CEO OF SPRINGFIELD REMANUFACTURING CORP. (SRC)

Through a unique management system called the Great Game of Business,
SRC is now run by the employees, with the CEO as referee.

PAGE 140

ANITA RODDICK  GROUP MANAGING DIRECTOR OF THE BODY SHOP INTERNATIONAL

By bringing humanity back into business,
The Body Shop has aroused feelings of enthusiasm and commitment among its staff
more common to a political movement than a corporation.

PAGE 155

DON BURR  CEO OF PEOPLE EXPRESS AIRLINES INC.

One of the fastest-growing companies in history was also the most revolutionary
in people management—All employees were owners, managers and jack-of-all-trades.

PAGE 165

HARRY QUADRACCI  CEO OF QUAD/GRAPHICS INC.

Working at Quad/Graphics, employees get more than just a job; they get an education.

PAGE 174

JAN CARLZON 6 CEO OF SCANDINAVIAN AIRLINES SYSTEM GROUP

To save SAS, Carlzon knew he had to change its culture. He had to remove the fear
and allow mistakes in order to inspire success.

PAGE 181

If you were to put 100 successful company founders in a room and ask them to talk openly and honestly about what makes them toss and turn at night, the answers from each might surprise you. Yes, you might hear mention of aggressive Asian competitors or onerous federal regulations or possibly, uncontrollable health-care costs, but the majority will talk about their company's "people problems."

Survey after survey shows that CEOs are the least confident about and the most challenged by managing people issues. And it's perfectly understandable—few company leaders are trained to be managers. They might be spectacular retailers or gurus of technology, but when it comes to communicating the company's goals, making demands, expressing their expectations of employees, many don't know where to begin and others simply don't even try. Company leaders can make mistakes all the time, either by misreading signals or by falsely assuming that osmosis is a perfectly acceptable form of company communications.

Managing People is not just one of the business disciplines, like Marketing or Finance. It is the foundation upon which all disciplines function. The best marketing plan in the world won't bring in the revenues if your sales force is demoralized. Manufacturing excellence can't be realized if your workers behave like the living dead. It's questions such as the following that managers face on a day-to-day basis and, if addressed properly, can be the engine upon which your company moves forward.

- Let's say you have an employee who has been with your company from the beginning, done a great job over the years, received decent pay raises to reward that work, but is now making more money than your more recently hired vice-president, whose work for the company is 10 times more valuable. How do you compensate and keep motivating your long-term employee without giving him more money?

- What do you do with an employee who performs his job well, but has such a bad attitude that it is demotivating all the people who have to work with him? Can you let someone go simply for having a bad attitude?

• How can you address the inescapable feeling you've got that your company is staffed by too many doing too little? What kind of incentive plan can you devise for the company to get people motivated, invested, and more productive?

These are the challenges, CEOs tell us, that cause sleepless nights. And these are the challenges this book is meant to address. No nouveau management theories or hypothetical discussions. Instead, we've assembled 101 ideas that have been developed and put to the test in leading small companies throughout the country.

Most of the material in this book originally appeared in the pages of *Inc.* magazine, in a section called "Hands On: Ideas and Resources for Growing a Business." Since its founding in 1979, *Inc.* has written for and about small to midsize companies. Its mission has been to provide management advice, inspiration, and a sense of community to the owners and top managers of growing businesses.

In addition to its "Hands On" information, *Inc.* has consistently showcased the practices of innovators in leadership and human resource development. This book contains frank discussions with six of these leaders, who argue that the extraordinary achievements in their organizations are due, in large part, to the original approaches they take to managing people. These interviews originally appeared in *Inc.*, where the willingness of the CEOs to express their failures as well as their achievements, made them one of the magazine's most popular features. The CEOs are:

Jack Stack of Springfield Remanufacturing Corp., who describes The Great Game of Business, in which every employee is informed about every aspect of the company's performance and is thus able to contribute to all decisions and share in all the risks and rewards.

Anita Roddick of The Body Shop, whose worldwide network of stores depends upon superb training and communications that keep people motivated and focused despite being, in some cases, half a world away from company headquarters.

Ken Iverson of Nucor Steel, who, wanting to increase productivity and minimize turnover, created a compensation system that is now admired and copied by companies large and small.

Harry Quadracci of Quad/Graphics, whose willingness to try out new ideas—everything from a three-day workweek to employee-run entrepreneurial ventures—has created a company consistently voted one of the 100 best companies in America to work for.

Donald Burr of People Express Airlines, who conducted one of the most radical experiments in people management over the past decade. Though no longer in business, it is ironic that People Express, the fastest-growing airline in history, is now one of the most studied management models anywhere in the country.

Jan Carlzon of Scandinavian Airlines, who is one of the great modern-day practitioners of good people management, as well as the most eloquent spokesperson for the values and philosophies that must exist in a company before techniques can be applied effectively.

One final note about the format of this book. The 101 ideas appear one per page and are divided into 12 chapters, each of which deals with a different aspect of managing, from hiring to training, motivating to compensating, incentivizing to firing. While some ideas were prepared specifically for this book, others appear as they did originally in *Inc.* with some minor editing. Since the original publication of their stories, readers might note, some of the companies mentioned may have gotten larger, some smaller; a few, such as People Express, may no longer exist. Keep in mind that the items were chosen for the value of the ideas. They are meant to inform, but also inspire. Part of their appeal is that they are simple to understand, easy to apply or adapt, and in most cases, require little or no resources. Some of the ideas generated more interest or were more frequently copied by *Inc.*'s 2.2 million readers than others. These we've highlighted with a stamp called "Reader's Choice.".

"When you're hiring,
you want people who love you and
love the values of your company.
You don't want confrontation all
the time. Also you don't want
people who just have a sense of
their own growth, not others'
or the company's."

ANITA RODDICK

GROUP MANAGING DIRECTOR OF THE BODY SHOP

Etch-a-Sketch Job Descriptions

After starting their own company, OurTown Television Productions, right out of college, Steven Rosenbaum and his partner couldn't offer prospective employees the kind of salaries that local stations paid. So OurTown **offered something else: jobs custom-tailored to workers' tastes. As a result, staffers made less money, but most of them loved their jobs.**

Rosenbaum's accommodating approach is still manifest in almost every one of the 18 positions at his Saratoga Springs, N.Y., company. OurTown's story coordinator, for example, is also the staff welder because he told Rosenbaum he loved welding. Rosenbaum spends a lot of time finding out what employees love and hate about their jobs and trying to eliminate or reduce the distasteful responsibilities. Usually that means identifying someone else in the company who's interested in the task.

Still, all employees have to do something they're not particularly fond of. And creating a perfectly tailored job for a new hire can sow dissatisfaction among employees. Rosenbaum waived company policy and allowed a new producer-reporter to do her own voice-over recording on her stories. Then three other reporters on staff wanted to do their own voice-overs, as well. Rosenbaum asked them to come back to him in six months if they still felt strongly about it. "The easy solution would be to make an ironclad rule with no exceptions," he says. "But I look at it as having three people on staff who would like to build their skill level."

Granted, some people can get lost in this kind of environment, but the payoff for the headaches is that Rosenbaum retains many employees who could work elsewhere for better pay. He says productivity is also higher. He estimates OurTown produces TV programs with one-half to two-thirds the staff other production companies require. OurTown's revenues have spurted from $600,000 in 1989 to an estimated $1.1 million for 1991. The best part: his flexibility costs him nothing but his time and interest in keeping employees happy. Can he continue doing that as his company grows? He's working on it.

Bull's-Eye Recruiting

After tiring of the erratic response to newspaper ads and the exorbitant costs of recruitment agencies, Steve Desautel, vice-president of Accu Bite Dental Supply Inc. in East Lansing, Mich., **decided to "market" his company's job openings himself. And he did just that, using a time-honored marketing technique—direct mail.**

Desautel needed to hire people with technical backgrounds to understand and sell his company's dental products. The customers to whom they would be selling are principally dental assistants, hygienists, and lab technicians. So putting two and two together, he reasoned, why not hire the people who use the products? Desautel knew, however, that he couldn't simply hire away his customers' employees without losing customers in the process. So he tried another route.

By obtaining the membership lists of local professional organizations and a list of licensed professionals from the state regulatory agency, Desautel goes directly to the target prospects at their home rather than their business addresses. His mailings include a description of the company, the job offerings, and the qualifications required. If the prospect is interested or knows of someone else who might be, she can write in to request an application. On average, Accu Bite sends out 500 letters and receives a 5% to 6% response.

Desautel has used this recruiting method four times now with great success. After sales training, the new recruits are paying for themselves after only five weeks on the job. The cost of the mailings, including production and postage, are cheaper than the cost of a classified ad in the local paper. And, of course, there is also the intangible benefit of giving the company more exposure to potential future clients.

Besides saving money, Desautel has also been able to make money as a result of this technique. With each search, the mailing lists become more and more fine-tuned, so much so that Accu Bite has now begun renting them to non-competitors.

Classified Information

Linda L. Miles gets plenty of hard workers to reply to her help-wanted ads. The CEO of Linda L. Miles & Associates, a $1.2-million trainer of medical office support staff, in Virginia Beach, Va., has fine-tuned her ad copy over the past five years while hiring 16 people. "When employees have a bad day at work, they go home and scan the want ads. Appeal to their sense of being underappreciated," recommends Miles, whose hook reads: "Are you enthusiastic, caring, and dependable? Would you enjoy a secretarial opportunity in an office that truly appreciates the staff?" "That says the company respects employees," says Miles.

She now recommends the approach to her clients. One doctor **changed his ads from focusing on benefits, hours, and salary to a more appreciative approach.** His responses shot up from 6 to 100. "His old ads attracted applicants who were more interested in benefits than doing a great job," says Miles.

Don't Ask!

With discrimination lawsuits on the rise and labor law becoming more labyrinthian, interviewing job candidates is getting trickier all the time. Small companies stumble more often than most, according to Stephen Cabot, a partner at Harvey, Pennington, Herting & Renneisen, in Philadelphia. One of the most common mistakes? "Asking questions on the no-no list," says Cabot.

It's the innocent, getting-to-know-you queries that can get an employer into trouble. Some key examples of what not to ask:

"So, when did you graduate from high school?" People usually offer this kind of information voluntarily on a resume, but if they don't, don't ask. It could be construed as revealing a bias against job applicants of a certain age.

"Will you be taking time off from work to observe Passover?" The question is valid because it is job-related. But the wording is inappropriate. Instead, ask, "Will the times of your religious observances conflict with the regular work periods at this company?"

"Have you ever been convicted of a crime?" Cabot says the question is too broad. Zero in on offenses that are pertinent to the job. Of someone applying to be a bank teller, for example, you'd ask about crimes relating to theft. *Never* ask about arrests, because they're not an indication of wrongdoing.

"Are you in good health?" The classic application-form question is, indeed, a no-no. "One can ask only about physical or mental impairments if they would limit an applicant's ability to do the job," explains Cabot.

"Finding good child care is so hard. Do you have any baby-sitting problems?" This inquiry is OK if you consistently ask it of *both* male and female applicants—and you can prove it. Otherwise it smacks of sex discrimination.

"I see you've spent a lot of time in Paris. Were you born there?" You can't ask if someone is a citizen of another country. You can ask about U.S. citizenship or if an applicant has the legal right to work in this country.

Reach Out

When your line of business is out of line with your region's industrial base, finding skilled employees is nearly impossible. Karmak Inc., which manufactures software for the trucking industry, is located in Carlinville, Ill., far from any hub of the high-tech universe. As a consequence, local help-wanted ads for software-savvy employees bombed.

Desperate to build his staff, CEO Richard Schien appealed to the families and friends of prospective employees. **"Do you know someone with these skills who would like to move to the area?" his new help-wanted ads read.**

"Many people would love to live in the area but think there wouldn't be work for them," says Schien. "This extends the reach of the local papers." Schien ran the ad each week for seven months and filled 15 positions as a result.

Analyzing Behavioral Traits

A good many 'once burned, twice shy' CEOs believe that the single, **most important ingredient to hiring well is writing an accurate job description.**

At Advanced Network Design, a third-party telecommunications handler in La Mirada, Calif., managers begin by writing down a list of actions a person will undertake in the job. Then they itemize the behavior necessary to execute those activities successfully. Finally, they concoct a script for the interview: "You write open-ended questions that will get people to discuss their previous work history in such a way as to disclose whether they have those traits," explains Dave Wiegand, the company's president.

The conventional job description focuses on activities. For example, a description for a salesperson might read—generate and close new sales, make 15 cold calls a week, write call reports. There is nothing inaccurate about this definition, but as Wiegand points out, it leaves you clueless to find someone who will be a good salesperson, it only helps to identify candidates who have done those activities before.

In contrast, Wiegand's job description for a salesperson consists of 17 behavioral traits. One of them is healthy "self-talk", the mental dialogue we have with ourselves. To uncover this characteristic, Wiegand might ask applicants what they would say to a fellow salesperson who was getting a lot of rejections and few appointments. However they respond may be an indication of how they motivate themselves. What he wants to hear is a buck-up-and-keep-going speech, which he believes is a key predictor of a salesperson's success.

One way to start constructing truly useful job descriptions is to itemize the patterns of behavior of your most successful employee in each job category. Then revise that list as you get better at hiring.

READER'S CHOICE

Temporary Until Proven Otherwise

"The biggest nightmare is running an ad and having hundreds of people respond, most of whom are not qualified," says Larry Victor, president of Victor Business Systems, an instant-office service in Memphis.

After a great deal of experimentation, Victor has hit upon a low-risk hiring technique. When he has an opening, he contacts several of the five temporary-help agencies he's established relationships with. They recruit and screen according to his specifications and send over three to five candidates, and Victor picks one. If he likes the way the temporary staffer works out, he hires him or her permanently.

Because Victor **observes the placement agencies' rules—waiting until after the three-month no-hiring period is up—he doesn't have to pay a placement fee to the agency.** In the meantime, of course, he's had ample time to assess the temporary worker's skills and fit with the company.

Victor typically continues shelling out the same amount for the employee, but because the agency no longer collects its cut, the employee gets a fatter paycheck. "We're able to find more qualified people faster," claims Victor.

Hiring in Bulk

In a fast-growth company, hiring all the necessary people at one time can be a daunting experience. Adina Marcheschi, of CPS Employment Services Network Inc., decided that **the most time-efficient solution would be to hold a company open-house.**

In the past, this head-hunting firm in Westchester, Ill., had gone the normal route—an ad in the paper—with mixed results. "A lot of times when people called in response to our ad, they'd say they weren't interested as soon as I mentioned the word *commission*," Marcheschi says. Yet she knew that visitors often fell in love with the company's young, open environment. So she had a display ad designed for the local paper that included an invitation and a small map with directions. The ad requested RSVPs, so CPS could follow up on those who did not show up. Marcheschi also made the ad into flyers, which were sent to local graduate schools and continuing-education programs. Finally, a letter was sent to families of each employee, knowing that some of the best hires are often found close to home.

Marcheschi believes that approaching the hiring process this way attracted people who may not have responded to a conventional ad. At the open house, 60 prospects were given an company introduction, watched a video, and each was briefly interviewed by a manager. Since all the managers were present for the open house, they would often refer some applicants to others for further screening if necessary. Also, as part of the screening process, each applicant was asked to suggest other people they knew who might be interested in the company. This request yielded even more prospects—and good ones.

All told, the ad and the open house brought in more than 100 applicants, 5 of whom were ultimately hired. The process itself saved the managers time and was so successful that next year CPS plans to stage an open house for two nights.

Sidestepping the Potholes in Employee Leasing

One of the most enticing ways to save money and reduce paperwork these days is by contracting with an employee-leasing company. For a fee, such companies will become your human-resources-administration department, handling all your payroll, insurance and benefits. The employee-leasing company becomes the coemployer of your workers, and you get better programs at a price you could never negotiate on your own. But the employee-leasing field is so new and is growing so fast that it has attracted some undesirable participants. **Here are the questions you should ask to find an honest, well-run employee-leasing company:**

Could I have the name of your bank, your insurance broker, and your insurance company? You should request credit references from the bank, details on the insurance coverage provided, and duration of the relationship with the insurance company. Check also that the insurance company is highly rated by A. M. Best.

Who is your third-party administrator (TPA)? Employee-leasing companies that are self-insured, as most are, must have an independent company, or TPA, handle administrative matters and claims payouts. Ask the TPA for a record of the leasing firm's payments of claims and a description of any cash-flow problems, and—most important—if the firm has ever asked the TPA to stop paying claims.

Is your administrator licensed to sell insurance in my state? If your leasing company is using a self-insured health plan, the TPA or the reinsurer must be licensed in the employee's state. Check with your state insurance commissioner's office.

How do you handle sexual-harassment charges? Sexual harassment is a joint liability of the leasing company and its client. A good company has a comprehensive approach which may include training programs in sensitivity, safety, and other areas.

What kind of reinsurance coverage do you have? The self-insured firm must have an insurance company that will step in if an individual claim or all claims in aggregate surpass a specified figure. Otherwise, you won't be adequately covered against catastrophe.

As always, with any relationship of this sort, ask for audits and client references.

Test-Driving Job Applicants

Silver-tongued and disarming, salespeople can be the most vexing job applicants to assess. Dazzlers can talk their way into a job but may not bring in revenues. Advanced Network Design (AND), a third-party telecommunications handler in La Mirada, Calif., **designed two "activity" tests to discern the verbally competent from the truly skilled.**

Toward the end of a lengthy interview in a conference room, Dave Wiegand, AND's president, gives the candidate an assignment. "I'm going back to my office," he says, "I want you to call me from the conference room, pretend I'm a potential customer, and try to set up an appointment." Then Wiegand turns on his speakerphone and waits in his office with two colleagues.

He's looking for answers to three questions. First, is the salesperson honest? "The worst way to start a new sales process is to lie to a secretary and say that the potential customer knows why the salesman is calling," says Wiegand. Second, does the salesperson go after the goal? After being turned down, many salespeople segue into a sales pitch. Wrong move, says Wiegand. Finally, is the applicant persistent? Wiegand makes the applicant ask for the appointment at least three times.

The second test is designed to give Wiegand a feeling for the person's selling style. Wiegand gives the applicant the specifications of two products. Then he asks the candidate to sell him one over the other. Wiegand doesn't care which product is chosen, but he does want to know the salesperson's selection rationale, as well as his or her sales strategy. Wiegand also observes how the salesperson handles objections and adapts to unexpected developments.

The tests make it easy to eliminate weak contenders. But they also help unearth candidates who excel at selling, though they may be only mediocre at interviewing.

Morning, Noon, and Night

Some folks are morning people, some come to life at night, and others are bubbly all day. **If you're in the service business, you want people who have a high energy level all day long. So, how do you find them?**

Barry Steinberg, president of $4-million Direct Tire Sales, a retail store in Watertown, Mass., always conducts three interviews with prospective employees on three separate days. One meeting takes place in the evening, a second at midday, and a third in the morning. "I get an indication of their energy level at all hours," says Steinberg. "I want people who are good with customers throughout the day."

Keeping the Pipeline Full

Fuchs Copy Systems, in West Allis, Wis., sells copiers. But as anyone who's ever confronted a broken-down copier can tell you, the important thing about a copier isn't how you buy it. It's how fast it can be fixed. So Jim Fuchs's company lives or dies on the strength of his 30 service people.

When a member of Fuchs's service team became sick or left the company, replacing him was tough. So to attract potential service technicians, he **developed an apprenticeship program for area high school and college students. Periodically, he runs a "career night" and also donates copiers to the schools' workshops, so students can work on them.** Students accepted into the apprentice program can work during the summer or part-time.

To give them a taste of the business, apprentices were assigned an especially messy job: rebuilding the developer units of the copiers. It was a brilliant move. The senior technicians, who previously would have had to rebuild a developer at the customer's work site, could now simply insert an already-renovated unit. That cut servicing time and improved the company's workmanship. It also forced the shop to become much more organized about figuring out benchmarks for the apprentices to hit.

Fuchs captured the pool of technical people he needed. On average he's made one permanent hire per year for the past five years—and not one has left. "The best hires," says Fuchs, "have a preexisting relationship with you that allows for more evaluation on both sides than an interview does."

The Art of Hiring Professional Temps

In theory, the widespread availability of temporary professional workers is a small-business owner's dream come true. You can hire everyone from cost accountants to road-and-tunnel engineers for as long as you need them. When your special project is finished, those temps conveniently disappear. And with professional temps, "there's enough do-it-on-their-own attitude that I can assign a task and not worry about it being done," says Peggy Brown, accounting manager of software publisher Aldus Corp., in Seattle.

When selecting a temp-help company for professional workers, consider the following:

Is it really a temporary-help company, or is it an executive-search operation? If it's the latter, your "temporary" worker may not qualify as an independent contractor under Internal Revenue Service rules. Also a temporary-help company can usually fill a position much more quickly than an executive-search company can.

Make sure the company has been in business for a while. A seasoned firm should be able to guarantee an immediate replacement if you're not happy with the professional it sends over. If a temp will be working with proprietary information, will he or she sign a confidentiality agreement? Look also for a firm that specializes in the discipline you're seeking. Its placement counselors should themselves have experience in your particular field.

Next, turn your attention to the quality of the firm's temporaries. The firm should have checked previous jobs, references, and other credentials.

When it comes time to use a temporary, beware of the pitfalls. Aldus's Brown says she felt that temps placed an extra burden on her. "In a fairly long-term assignment you usually don't find out what a temporary can really do until a significant amount of time has elapsed," she says. "As a manager I'm taking more time to do stuff that I would delegate if I had a permanent worker."

And though temporaries are generally cheaper than regular employees, there can be hidden costs. Brown says overtime costs, which she wouldn't incur with a permanent employee, can add substantially to the bill. In a tight market, it's worth trying to negotiate a cheaper rate.

Their Loss is Your Gain

Outplacement is thriving given the rash of plant consolidations and work reductions nationwide. Small companies that take the trouble to **plug into these corporate outplacement centers can find a rich source of seasoned, professional job candidates**—without having to pay heavy recruitment costs. At no cost, small companies can list their employment openings with the centers and attend company-sponsored job fairs.

For some of those out of work, the idea of joining a small business can be especially appealing, says Russ Creason, a Detroit-based outplacement consultant. "These [job candidates] see the potential for more professional freedom and a chance to get away from the politics and structure of a larger company." Moreover, adds Creason, if a small company is a supplier to a large corporation, or wants to be one, "signing up one of their former employees makes good sense."

Dennis Robichaud, a senior electronics engineer at Prospective Computer Analysts Inc., in Bedford, Mass., listed openings for two engineering jobs at the placement office of a *Fortune* 500 company that had announced layoffs. By dealing with the outplacement center, he figures he has already saved $6,000, the amount he would normally pay to an executive search firm. "We then have the option of offering a higher salary" to the desirable candidates, Robichaud says. "That gives us, as a small company, an edge over the rest of the market."

14

The Team Approach

Terri and Steve Cowan, co-owners of Professional Salon Concepts (PSC), based in Joliet, Ill., were content to hire one person at a time, as the need arose, until they were faced with sudden turnover, last year. They needed to hire four people at once, all of whom would then be tied up with in-house training from 30 to 90 days. The small crisis persuaded Terri to revamp her recruiting and hiring process.

First , she instituted the commonly-used practice of referral bonuses, giving an employee a bonus for every recruit referred to her who is ultimately hired and stays with the company. But beyond that, Terri **changed the interviewing process to get everyone in the company more involved and invested in the hiring process. She has set up a system of team interviews.**

Terri organizes her 15 consultants and 5 department heads into 5 teams. After Terri has interviewed all referrals, she asks back the best candidates for team interviews. Starting at 5 P.M., each candidate is interviewed for 20 minutes by each team. Every interviewer ranks the candidate on a list of the 20 to 25 attributes that PSC is looking for. After the marathon interviewing session, the grades are tallied, and the highest-ranking candidates are asked back to be interviewed by Terri and Steve.

Using this approach, Terri finds her consultants much more enthusiastic about the new hires. Previously, she found herself "selling" her new hires to employees, who were often skeptical. Now the teams have a vested interest in seeing the new person succeed—so much so that training new hires now seems effortless to Terri because everyone else is being so helpful.

"People know that we, as a country, have gone from net lender to net borrower. They've gotten the message that they have to be very well trained in their profession so that if anything happens to their city or their company, they can go somewhere else."

JOHN MCCORMACK

CHAIRMAN OF VISIBLE CHANGES INC.

First Impressions

No one joins a company with a bad attitude. New employees come in wide-eyed and bushy-tailed. And the best welcome that many companies can muster? Forms to fill out, directions to the photocopier, and keys to the rest room.

An employee's first day is worth putting a little more thought into. Rosenbluth Travel, in Philadelphia, has **developed an imaginative two-day orientation that every company can learn from.** Here are some of the program's key components:

• A theme. This is your chance to convey a consistent vision of your company. At Rosenbluth, the ideal is "elegant customer service"—attentiveness to the customer that's beyond the call of duty. To illustrate it, a company trainer asks a group of new hires to come up with an example of a truly awful service experience they've had. Then, they're asked to define and act out the improvements that would warrant a good rating and those that would constitute elegant service.

• A symbol or slogan. You tread close to the abyss of corniness with this one, we know. But a motto can actually be an effective way to amplify your company's goals, provided (I) it's in harmony with all the other messages on the company airwaves, and (2) it's true.

Though it sounds like a cheerleader's mantra, Rosenbluth's "Live the Spirit" rings true to Kristen Mores, a Boston-based travel agent who went through the company's orientation last spring. "Everyone does help each other," she says. Warning: nothing turns a slogan into a punch line for a joke faster than insincerity. You and your top managers have to walk your talk.

• Respect. Surely everyone who comes into your company deserves not only your respect but also your gratitude and a few minutes of your complete attention. Hal Rosenbluth makes a ceremony out of this by serving high tea to new employees. You don't have to be so formal, but aim for an act that's memorable and demonstrates your personal interest. It might be as simple as pointing to a stack of resumes and saying, "Rich, we had 150 people apply for this job, but you were by far the best candidate. Here's why. . . ."

I See What You Mean

"We'd lecture employees all day long about what needed to be improved, and they wouldn't get it," recalls Mark Taylor, CEO of AFS Window & Door Corp., a $10-million maker of wooden windows and doors based in Anaheim, Calif. Now Taylor has meetings every two months in which he **serves pizza to his 70 employees and they watch videos of customers pointing out problems** with the windows on the construction sites. Since the sessions began, customer complaints have been cut by more than 60% and returns due to poor shipping and handling have become rare.

Salespeople, who double as camera-crew members, report that customers are flattered to have their complaints addressed so responsibly. "Employees immediately see how mistakes can cause problems and know what needs to be done," says Taylor.

READER'S CHOICE

17

Getting New Recruits on Track

Suppose your company is small enough that an official orientation program for new hires seems too expensive, yet it's large enough that fresh employees can get lost. Try an approach like the one used by Infincom, a Phoenix-area office-equipment distributor. Mike Koether, Infincom's president, **assigns every new employee the same task: seek out and have a one-to-one discussion with each of the top managers in the company within the first five days on the job.** The recruits gets a first-hand account of what will be expected of them and each manager's role in the company. The managers can assess the skills and resources being brought into the company. Most important, everyone gets to make the kind of personal connection that begets a strong sense of responsibility.

"We think the first 90 days of the employment relationship is the most critical time and establishes the entire foundation for the future," explains Koether. By taking great pains to see that new employees understand the company and their role in it, Koether keeps turnover and firing low.

The orientation assignment also serves as an early-warning system for wayward employees. If someone doesn't have the initiative to carry it out, says Koether, "we know that recruit is going to have a problem." The employee's manager maps out a 90-day action plan to help the employee understand what it will take to succeed.

18

What Is It That You Do?

Cross-training is a time-tested method of preparing employees to do more than one job. But Jim Baka, president of CERAC, a specialty chemical manufacturer in Milwaukee, also uses it to communicate the company's operations and goals.

"Several years ago, we started involving production managers in day-to-day sales and marketing decisions by having them sit in on meetings. We also sent them to trade shows. Our **goal was to make sure employees understood the way the work they do fits into our complete business operation and long-term goals**," says Baka.

Baka doesn't think it's too costly to teach employees skills they won't be using over the long term. "If I send my production plant manager to a two-day trade show, he'll come away understanding more about our customers and the need for meeting quality and scheduling goals than he could ever learn from me just talking at him."

Bottom-line results at the 120-employee company support Baka's theories: "Thanks to cross-training, we've been able to push sales up 15% to 20% per year, while maintaining a high quality of product, delivery performance, and technical customer assistance."

Putting Training to Use

The problem with most sales training is that it often lasts for an intense two or three days, then it's over. There's no guarantee that what's learned will be put into practice. That's why Ian Davison, CEO of Octocom Systems, **sends his salespeople to a training program that's spread out over several months and includes specific tasks for homework assignments.**

Why add tension when salespeople are already under the gun to meet their quotas? Davison believes his salespeople get more out of the training. "Their senses are sharpened, and they retain more," professes the head of the $37-million data-communications-systems manufacturer in Chelmsford, Mass. Perhaps more important, "what they learn is put to immediate use."

Under a system known as K Training (so named for its founder, Gustav Kaser) participants act out sales scenarios and work on certain approaches (closing techniques, for example) through role playing and one-on-one coaching. Homework might mean trying out, say, a new way to "turn complaints around" during actual sales calls, then reporting back to the class. The program also includes instruction on time management, etiquette, and communication skills (such as writing better letters).

About 12 of the 15 salespeople at Octocom have been through K Training, which consists of five one-day sessions over a period of three months. And the payoff has been evident. One junior salesman improved his performance dramatically by using silence and counter-objection techniques he had learned. The beauty of the approach, says Davison, is that "it's continual and self-checking."

In-House Customer Service

Before Paul Berg's employees could improve their service to customers, they needed to learn how to communicate better with one another. To get them talking, Berg, CEO of Enterprise Builders, asked them to conduct a little internal market research.

During a company picnic, Berg handed each of the 13 employees at his $18-million, Avon, Conn., construction company written instructions that asked them to consider themselves "customers" of one another. Each employee went around to the others one at a time and asked them to list their 10 greatest needs as a customer. They then agreed on an action plan to meet each need. Later, employees looked at all the responses they'd gathered, identified those needs mentioned most frequently, and made them immediate goals. They also agreed to meet in a month to discuss progress on the problems.

Says Berg, **the exercise "sanctioned workers to identify what didn't work right and to fix it instead of excusing it as 'the ways things are done.'"** During the exercise, senior project manager Steve Buccheri heard about a lot of frustration with the job-cost reporting system. So he worked with six users to develop a better model, then brought it to the accounting department. The improved system is now in place.

Berg expects a big payoff in time. "In our business, there are so many levels of customers—the subcontractors, the architects, the owners. I wanted our people to understand service in a living and personal way, so we started on the inside, and we'll work our way out to every layer of customers."

Overcoming Illiteracy

"Who wants to be the first person to raise his hand and say he can't read?" asks Roland S. Boreham Jr., chairman and CEO of Baldor Electric Co., headquartered in Fort Smith, Ark. So to coax workers in Baldor's Columbus, Miss., plant into an on-site literacy program, Boreham **used video testimonials from six employees who had the courage to participate in the program and tell others how it helped them learn to read.** Boreham used an employee interviewer and one VHS video camera to shoot the testimonials.

About 25% of the 350 workers in Columbus enrolled in the program. "The messages really hit home," says Boreham, who expects fewer mistakes on the company's electrical-motor assembly lines because more employees can read manuals, job specifications, and invoices.

An In-House Sales School

In a hurry to get newly hired salespeople into their territories and selling? The rush may be costing your company more than you know in lost sales and in sales-force turnover. At Paychex Inc., a $120-million national supplier of payroll and other business services, **every new salesperson goes through seven weeks of training before even meeting a prospect.** The result: new hires start earning more than their draw twice as fast as before, and turnover has fallen dramatically.

Gene Polisseni, vice-president of marketing, calculates that Paychex spends $3,500 per trainee to operate a professionally staffed school at the company's Rochester, N.Y., headquarters. That amount includes instructors' salaries as well as transportation, housing, and meals for the trainees. It may seem like a lot, says Polisseni, but it's a lot less than the roughly $18,600 it costs Paychex to recruit and train a replacement for a salesperson who gets fired or quits.

The thinking behind the Paychex approach is that every salesperson first has to understand the company's products. Consequently, during the first three weeks of the Paychex school, the 16 or so students that start every month take courses on tax laws and accounting principles, and study the services that Paychex sells. After three weeks the students take a comprehensive exam. If they don't pass, they go home to look for another job. Those who pass are sent to work for two weeks at a Paychex operations branch to learn firsthand what the company does. They also accompany branch salespeople on calls, but only to watch and listen. In the last week, it's back to Rochester for more classroom work, now, finally, on selling skills. Only after graduation does the new salesperson get to solo on an actual sales call.

Even if you can't afford a full-blown sales school, Polisseni contends, whatever time you can spend teaching your salespeople about your company's specific products or services can help them get up to speed faster in the field. "Training is an investment that a progressive company can't afford not to make," he says.

"I don't want people
to sit there and passively accept
leadership. I want them
to become active in leadership,
and that means giving them a
constructive path to follow.
I don't think management should
be a glorified cheerleader."

JACK STACK

CEO OF SPRINGFIELD REMANUFACTURING CORP.

A No-Door Policy

Downsize. Slash costs. Work harder. Lessons from the recession don't send your spirits tap-dancing. After revenues and head count fell by a devastating 25% at Chaix & Johnson, an L.A.-based design firm, everyone began wondering whether the business would survive. Not the sort of thinking that leads to a sprightly recovery, decided Scott Kohno, a managing director.

He tried a lot of things to reenergize his 30 employees, but the most effective change was simple: he **moved out of his office with its 18-foot ceiling and into the middle of the work floor.** "It shocked everybody," recalls Kohno. At first, staffers made a joke out of it by marking imaginary walls on the floor around his desk with masking tape.

Kohno began to notice a remarkable change. His staff contact "is 100 times more frequent. There are a million little discussions that move the company 10 times faster," he explains. "The energy level has totally changed." His own involvement has intensified, too. "It's the difference between being on the basketball floor instead of the bleachers. You see the hysteria, the aggravation, the tension on faces, and you can appreciate it more. You don't see those beads of sweat any other way," contends Kohno.

Now less energy goes into hiding problems and more into solving them. Other benefits: no more closed-door meetings and vying for private offices. The disadvantages? "Well," says Kohno, speaking over the music from a coworker's boom box, "there's a lot of noise."

Spicing up the Boring Jobs

Many company owners can't make every job in their company interesting. Particularly if their product is inherently, well, *boring.* For example: How do you stimulate an employee who cuts 10-foot-long pieces of cable assembly all day?

That's what Randall Amon, CEO of ABL Electronics Corp., in Timonium, Md., wondered a few years ago. His solution: field trips. "By itself, our product just isn't very exciting. But if we can **take employees out of the plant and show them how our products are used** in a fetal monitoring device at a hospital, we can show them how their work fits into the world," says Amon.

He tries to arrange such jaunts once every six months for all his 46 employees. The trips have been surprisingly effective. "People have more pride in their work when they understand how our products are used," says Amon.

Making Teams Work

Say you're sold on all the buzzwords: empowerment, partnership, self-directed teams. **You've flattened your organization by eliminating middle managers. You've created teams with direct customer involvement. Then you sit back, waiting for the organization to take off at warp speed.**

That's when you find out the truth about granting power: not everybody wants it. "Some people like to come to work and be told what to do," says Tom Pechacek, president of Displaymasters, a designer and builder of trade show exhibits. While the company, based in New Hope, Minn. aims to hit $10 million in revenues this year thanks to its new team-oriented organization implemented a year ago, many of the team members resisted their new role.

A simple exercise used by Ann Marie Fasching, leader of Displaymasters' customer service team, helped her team members significantly. She had her team fill out a questionnaire made up of three questions—Why are we a team? What do you expect from your team leader? What do you expect from your team members?

Responding to the first question allowed everyone to voice their concerns and essentially, buy into the new orientation. Responses to the second and third questions enabled the team to begin to establish new patterns of behavior. For example, under the old system, if any employee had a 'people problem' with another employee, the complainer might deposit the problem in her bosses' lap. Under the new system, the team decided, each person would be responsible for dealing with the 'problem' person on their own; the team leader could only be used for mediation if necessary.

Since completing the questionnaire, Fasching's team has gone on to tackle stiffer challenges. Three of Fasching's team members who sometimes feel "trapped" by their jobs—including the person who answers calls from complaining customers—have embarked on a job-sharing schedule in which they rotate jobs every day.

Wall-to-Wall Carping

In a poll conducted in 1991 among several hundred corporate members of the American Productivity & Quality Center (APQC), a nonprofit business-research organization in Houston, more than half the respondents (56.8%) said they worked in fully walled offices, while less than a quarter (21.4%) claimed modular settings. The nearly three-to-one ratio suggests that semiwalled workplaces are not gaining on closed-door tradition as rapidly as the office-decor trade may presume. Indeed, a number of respondents thought open or modular offices showed disregard for people, dispatching that opinion—the APQC was chagrined to note—in "strong language." Groused one, "Open offices reflect a 'cheap' attitude." An organization that implements them, another complained, "treats employees as cattle."

Why so snippety? Disaffection is likely to result, theorizes Dan Wiseman, an APQC-affiliated consultant on white-collar work settings, "if you impose an open office on people who don't perceive themselves as a team." When one company designed new open offices, it separated clerical people from the executives they supported. The physical and social isolation resulted in a marked *increase* in errors and delays. **After the company asked the employees to redo the office layout themselves, efficiency and morale soared.** "If office people are given a chance to create ownership of their own space," Wiseman observes, "they find ways to make it work."

Whatever Turns You On

Money and benefits are the universal carrots dangled before employees. But they can be ridiculously out of place. "Do you think you could stimulate Mother Teresa with a retirement plan?" asks Ron Parks, president of Millard Manufacturing, in Omaha.

After nearly 20 years of managing experience, Parks has devised an **interviewing technique that digs deep into workers' hearts and minds to figure out, among other things, what motivates them.** The information helps Parks select the right person for a job, but it's also an invaluable management tool.

The key question he asks to pinpoint a person's source of motivation: "When you are working on a project, how do you know you are doing a good job?" A person who tells you that she knows within herself whether her work is first-rate is, in Parks's term, "internal"—or self-directed. The person who says, "My boss (or my coworkers) tells me so" is external, requiring input from the outside.

Either may be a desirable worker in the right job. Obviously, an external would flounder in a position in which his work is rarely reviewed. Nor would he thrive working for a boss who is stingy with praise.

In contrast, praise is sometimes not the best tool with the self-directed. Such people will feel embarrassed—or even offended—if they are complimented by someone who isn't qualified to judge their accomplishments.

Parks, who has spent nearly two decades perfecting his "thinking model" of management, asks another dozen or so questions to ascertain an employee's performance profile. But if he could focus on one trait only, Parks would choose motivation. "I can accomplish more by knowing this one attribute than I can with any other," he explains.

Knowing Your Product Inside and Out

When you think of fun and games, assembling a fuel injector might not immediately come to mind. Not so at Diesel Technology Corp. (DTC), a $70-million fuel injector manufacturer in Wyoming, Mich. This company **used its principal product, which possesses absolutely no playful characteristics to speak of, to have some fun and educate its employees at the same time.**

At a company meeting, an employee stood up and said that he had been making plungers for 15 years and had no idea how they fit into the company's final product. DTC president Derek Kaufman immediately saw an opportunity for fun. After the meeting, he and some of his staff proceeded to take 50 fuel injectors apart. Each of the 30 or so parts for each injector was tagged with its name and function, and then all the parts were put into a bag unassembled.

At the next meeting, Kaufman challenged anyone that was interested to try to assemble a fuel injector on his or her own and learn the company's product, literally inside and out. He explained that there were 50 fuel injectors disassembled in bags that could be signed out on a library card basis and taken home for experimentation. Of the 550 employees at the company at the time, 505 showed up for the challenge.

The "I Got It Together" campaign, as it is called, has involved everyone—janitors, secretaries, accountants, production workers, and management—in understanding the complex nature of the product. After assembling the product, which on average takes 20 minutes to figure out, every employee is quizzed on each component's name and function. Upon successful completion, everyone gets an "I Got It Together" T-shirt. Ninety percent of the employees have now earned their shirts.

The program has been so popular, suppliers and customers have requested to sign out bags of parts themselves. Families of employees are also encouraged to "get it together." Kaufman brought a bag home to his 12-year-old son and challenged him to an assembly race. His son won hands-down, even beating the time of some of the on-line assembly workers. (Kaufman claims his son just has smaller fingers.)

Perking Up the Factory Floor

If office workers get fresh flowers, *you* get them too, CEO Chet Giermak promised line workers at Eriez Magnetics, a $55-million industrial-equipment manufacturer in Erie, Pa. The notion was greeted with blue-collar snickers. But once bunches of chrysanthemums started arriving regularly, the people on the floor took to them as positively as they had taken earlier to fine art hung on the walls, nameplates placed at workstations, and windows opening to the same landscaped outdoor views that upstairs executives were granted.

Mums were the latest inspiration in Giermak's determined **crusade to close the quality-of-work-life gap** between the company's 110 employees in engineering and sales, and its 145 factory employees. "I'm not saying everyone should have the same perks," he argues, "but I am saying that there are certain perks everybody should have." Hence production people, long since relieved of punching time clocks, also enjoy such white-collar advantages as long coffee breaks and access to corporate supplies for personal use.

Giermak shrugs off the extra and decidedly unconventional costs as mere "pocket money." No wonder: unexpected absenteeism is one-eighth the industry norm, and Eriez has practically no turnover—attributable, claims Giermak, to gaining equal respect from all 255 workers.

Second Founding

Scott Gibson likes a good party, but he decided to call Sequent Computer Systems' seventh anniversary bash a second founding. "We **wanted to get 1,300 people as charged up as the founding team,"** says Gibson, president of the $146-million Beaverton, Ore., company.

So Sequent posted billboards around town announcing the occasion, hired a band, and arranged to close off a few blocks in downtown Portland. The second founding featured a multi-media show, which included slides of employees and their kids and snatches of President John F. Kennedy's speech about sending a U.S. astronaut to the moon.

"It really worked—we had people crying at the end of this thing," Gibson says. And the new mission was clear: "We want to build a billion-dollar global company we can be proud of."

Safety First

Old work habits die hard. Sun Sportswear, a $73-million apparel company in Kent, Wash., counters the problem of getting employees to improve their work environment by letting them decide what needs to be done. **An employee-run safety committee**, comprising a rotating group of 12 volunteers from various departments, helps manage the company's environment by suggesting better ways to store hazardous materials and educating fellow employees on safety procedures. The group meets monthly; employees receive a paid day off for their services.

"The committee conducts a no-holds-barred tour of inspection and presents management with an informal report card," says chief operations officer Kaye Counts. "It's quite a service for the company and employees."

Making It Hard to Walk Away

"This is not a glamorous business," admits Richard Gaspari, president of the Richard Michael Group, a placement firm in Chicago. Turnover in the industry averages more than 40%. So keeping good people, he's decided, means keeping them interested, engaging them at their jobs and beyond. Gaspari does that with a **combination of bonuses and events that holds employee turnover down** to less than half the industry average. "Each month we've got something going on here," he says, "and every quarter something major going on—a party, a contest, or a trip."

Gaspari sponsors a few extravaganzas, like a trip to the Bahamas for top managers each spring, but he fills out the calendar with more imaginative, less expensive events:

• Guest speakers. Every month, Gaspari invites a speaker in to address the staff. Not every topic focuses on work-related matters—sometimes it gets personal. One recent guest spoke on crime prevention, a compelling subject for employees who often leave the downtown offices late at night.

• Dressing dollars. In any month when the company surpasses productivity goals, an office worker selected at random receives a $300 gift certificate to one of several shops good toward the purchase of a business suit. Gaspari wants people to dress professionally and believes the award delivers that message more tactfully than a dress code would.

• Spontaneous family dinners. Every few months or so, he treats the staff to dinner at a restaurant, no occasion necessary. Spouses and friends are invited. "People get to know one another at these dinners, and that's critical. That's another reason why they're not going to leave—they've made friends."

Gaspari spends about $75,000 on these events in a year—or about 2% of revenues. In five years the company's billings have grown from $268,000 to $3.8 million. "Some people believe in turnover, and they don't believe in what I'm doing," Gaspari says. "But to me, coming to work with the same people and getting to know them and their families is important."

"Before you reach an objective, you must be ready with a new one, and you must start to communicate it to the organization. But it is not the goal itself that is important. It's the fight to get there."

JAN CARLZON

CEO OF SCANDINAVIAN AIRLINES SYSTEM

For Whom the Bell Tolls

When Cable Technology Corp. (CTC) started operations last year, the charter group's founding idea was to be a world-class operation in every way, producing quality products and providing a quality work environment. To work toward this vision, the group came up with 14 principles the company would live by, one of which was very simple: Let people know when things happen.

Howard Kraye, part-owner and general manager of CTC, a high-tech electronics company in Albuquerque, **wanted to devise a method for instant communication, to broadcast good news or to discuss bad.** Someone suggested using a loudspeaker, which was rejected as too impersonal. Then someone mentioned a bell.

A few weeks later, Kraye installed, in the middle of the factory floor, a 200-pound school bell (circa 1890), which he painted gold. Now, whenever something good happens, any employee (or associate, as they are called) can walk over to the bell, ring it, and announce the news. News could range from a new contract, to bringing in a project under cost, to a defect-free order or a new baby. The bell is also used by Kraye to hold spontaneous "stand-up meetings" for company announcements.

Hardly a day goes by when the bell isn't rung at least once. Kraye has often wondered whether the enthusiasm of the bell-ringers would result in a Liberty Bell, complete with a giant crack. So far the bell is still in one piece, despite the company's spectacular growth, with $2.5 million in revenues in its first year of operation and a workforce that has gone from 14 to 72 associates.

What's on Your Plate This Week?

The president and CEO Anne Robinson, of Windham Hill Records, in Palo Alto, Calif., wants each employee to know how important his or her job is to the company. So she holds an hour-long meeting for all 30 employees at company headquarters every Monday morning at 9:00. **Everyone from the warehouse stocker to the chief executive herself gives a two-minute summary of what they have upcoming for the week.**

Why bother with such a production every week? It allows everybody in the company to report more accurate information than if a manager spoke for them, keeps the organization flat, and instills employees with a sense of pride in their work, reports Robinson.

Windham Hill's two branch offices also hold meetings. Minutes from the meetings are combined and circulated to all 60 employees. "Information is power, and I don't think it should live inside my head," says Robinson of the eight-year-old tradition that grew with the company.

Encouraging Suggestive Behavior

They once gathered ideas to make a business more prosperous. Today suggestion boxes mostly gather dust, ignored by employee and employer alike. Some CEOs we surveyed, however, are trying innovative ways to revive the tradition. Here are some of their suggestions:

• Make it easy—**You don't have to build a suggestion box per se.** Bryan Beaulieu, CEO of Skyline Displays, a tradeshow-exhibit manufacturer in Burnsville, Minn., relies on electronic mail. But the suggestion process doesn't happen of its own accord. To "prime the pump and break down barriers," Beaulieu pushes electronic correspondence at employee gatherings, encouraging all 220 workers to reach management's ear through the company's 100-terminal network.

• Change the concept—At Com-Corp Industries, a Cleveland metal stamper, president John Strazzanti has added "screwup boxes." "If we're doing something wrong, tell us," he urges employees. The resultant complaints are posted on the company bulletin board, along with management's responses.

• Provide a forum for follow-up—If receipt of a suggestion isn't acknowledged, good ideas are likely to drown in the well, notes Ray Otis, CEO of Hancock Information Group, a telemarketing company in Longwood, Fla. To encourage employees to expand on their initial insights, Otis discusses each suggestion at a monthly employee meeting. The result, says Otis: seeing that their views are taken seriously, workers can't wait to slip him their follow-up thoughts after the meeting.

• Stage a ceremony—Rewards for good suggestions don't have to be expensive, as Sequent Computer has proved. The Beaverton, Ore., manufacturer pays a token $10, dressing up the humble award with a battery of jokes and skits at an awards presentation. Recipients don't feel shortchanged, reports finance manager Ed Shearer, because the frolicsome fetes follow Sequent's work-is-fun philosophy. Which happens to be quite profitable: one $10 suggestion led to savings of $200,000.

Taking Stock

Gail Hering, CEO of Atmosphere Processing Inc., an automotive supplier in Holland, Mich., wanted to keep her employees up to date on the company's performance. She decided to **follow the model of public companies' annual shareholder meetings and instituted an annual jobholders' meeting.**

Since 1982 about 40% of the company's 180 employees have chosen to participate in the voluntary Saturday-morning event, a day that was picked because the factory is closed, the sales staff is off the road, and everyone has the opportunity to attend.

The group congregates in an off-site auditorium for about three hours to hear reports from key managers on standard public-company financials such as company profits, expenditures, investments, and strategies. Says Hering: "I'm a strong believer in the philosophy of 'The more employees know, the more valuable they are to the company.' These meetings show employees we aren't just paying lip service to how valuable their contribution is to this company."

READER'S CHOICE

Managing an At-Home Staff

The advantage of hiring people who work out of their homes is obvious: it's much cheaper—less office space, less equipment, and if they are independent contractors, no health benefit costs. But how do you know they aren't watching Oprah when they're supposed to be producing? And how do you get them to care about your company and its mission?

Jane Sandlar, president of Support Our Systems (SOS), says her 60 workers so appreciate working at home that she can be extremely demanding about the quality of their work. SOS, based in Red Bank, N.J., produces user guides for computer systems at large companies, so it relies on writers—a notoriously independent bunch. **To run her business largely on the steam of home workers, she has devised a system.** Here are the key points:

• Skill testing—Because employees won't be working at the office, you need to be sure they really can execute the work. Sandlar tests a prospective home worker's writing ability and study habits.

• Project orientation—Every document that SOS publishes is produced by a team headed by a project manager. That gives the writers a small group to identify with and a natural reason to communicate frequently.

• Multiple checkpoints—Though SOS's consultants can maintain whatever working hours they like, they are required to define them, to check in with SOS several times a day, and to have multiple means of electronic communication.

• Highly detailed assignments—SOS gives clients a clear picture of what their finished document will look like. That "design statement" also spells out consultants' assignments in detail. Frequent deadlines ensure that home workers are drawn into the production loop and can't ignore their responsibility to the company.

• Personalization—Sandlar meets with each consultant at least four times a year and is available at the office if needed. She also encloses a note with the paychecks, and schedules three companywide meetings a year.

• Frequent feedback—While consultants work on chapters of a document, their performance is continually being judged by a project manager. Sandlar gives every home worker a critique of every job.

The Week that Was

"In a small company everyone wears several hats," says William Barton, CEO of Overland Data Inc., a San Diego computer peripherals maker. "Since our early days we've **held weekly ExCom [executive committee] meetings to go over the financial health of the company."** Now the $7-million company has 53 employees, all welcome to attend the evening meetings. More than half do so regularly.

"When a company grows 40% annually, there are enough changes in a single week to make a significant impact on the company," says CFO Charlie Monts. Every meeting covers cash position, shipments, customer service reports, and production goals. "Employees know we aren't profitable every month," says Monts. "And they understand when we can't afford to buy supplies in volume or hire another person."

We Can Work It Out

Call it a corollary of fast growth: as sales multiply, so do disagreements between employees and managers. Formal **grievance procedures,** however, can often be expensive and time-consuming.

"We can't afford to let problems fester," states Michael Yag, CEO of Access TCA, a $4-million manufacturer of trade-show exhibits in Whitinsville, Mass. So at Access they take their beefs to the one truly private place at their offices in a converted mill: the tower.

Behind the large oak doors of the tower room, anyone can debate customer issues, hirings and firings, and employee reviews. The duelers don't come out until they agree on a course of action. "It's a nice way to air our differences and get on with what we have to do," says Yag.

Of course, there are other less medieval approaches to problem solving. American Steel & Wire, in Cuyahoga Heights, Ohio, hears complaints in a people's court. Other companies are training workers to be part-time mediators or ombudsmen. AT&T believes so firmly in ombudsmen that it employs a whole fleet of them.

Jump-starting Employee Confidence

It's one thing to rebuild your organization around employee participation. It's another to make your people like the new corporate style. A few years ago, an overhaul at Shepard Poorman, an Indianapolis printing company, was stuck. **Open communication among all workers was the goal. But employees at the company didn't like to speak out, and supervisors didn't enjoy hearing underlings' opinions.**

Drawing on his memory of a college psychology course, CEO Bob Poorman Jr. suspected the solution lay in bolstering his employees' self-esteem. Poorman hired the University of Indianapolis's training department to develop a class that would teach workers how to nurture relationships.

The program focuses on three fundamental topics—the self, relationships, and teamwork skills—and meets weekly. The most popular feature of the 18-week lecture series: in-class exercises that bring psychological theory to life. The routines vary from humorous exercises on hidden agendas to doing the hokey pokey in class to loosen people up. But such unlikely routines often trigger the most arresting insights. After being given a group assignment to draw a coat of arms for the company, recalls Don Curtis, formerly vice-president of quality: "I was so involved in drawing my vision of the perfect coat of arms that I forgot to include the group in deciding what should go into the drawing. It drove home the point about teamwork."

In the couple of years since the program started, almost half of Poorman's 330 employees have entered or completed the course. Their communication skills have improved so much that the company's management now lets customers speak directly to on-line workers about orders, instead of filtering inquiries through the sales department. More important, Poorman's work force seems to be gaining equanimity. Says benefits administrator Susan Rearick: "People accept criticism better—they see it as an insight."

Sunny Side Up

When managers of growing companies begin to focus on their own corners of the universe, camaraderie gets lost and communication mix-ups mount. Such was the case at Phoenix Textile Corp., a 56-employee institutional linens distributor based in St. Louis.

To stave off future miscommunications, CEO Palmer Reynolds began **hosting monthly breakfasts with the president.** She invites five different employees—one from each department—each month to join her at a local restaurant. "I learned how well we thought we were communicating and how much we weren't," Reynolds says.

"People get to know me. I get to know them. They get to know each other and, most important, what each other does," she says. On a recent morning outing, the sales department learned that the production department also had quotas to meet. As a result, the two groups ended a longstanding tug-of-war. Such direct communications have helped contribute to Phoenix's growth from $1.43 million to $24 million in six years.

Signed, Sealed, Delivered

People usually begin new jobs with great expectations. But the enthusiasm can fade long before managers are aware problems exist. One way to minimize the disillusionment, says Andy Plata, CEO of Computer Output Printing Inc. (COPI), a 23-employee laser printing specialist in Houston, is to develop ways of staying in touch with your workers. His approach: **have new employees write him letters.**

Before new people come to work at COPI, Plata and his managers ask them to write a letter to management about why they've chosen to work there. After the first week they're asked to write another letter describing "what they hope to accomplish at COPI and what contributions they feel they can make."

Seven weeks later they write a third letter detailing their progress. "We want to know if they're still turned on," says Plata. The letters become the focal point of managers' discussions about employee goals and how work relations can be improved.

He thinks new employees have adjusted to working at COPI more easily since he came up with the idea. "It helps us determine early how a person likes to work and what he or she needs from us."

Demystifying Strategy

Solar Press Inc., a $45-million direct-mail company in Naperville, Ill., looking for greater employee involvement, **took its business plan to the shop floor.**

In a one-day, off-site affair called Brain Day, the company confessed its yearly and long-range plans to its full-time employees.

During a two-hour morning session, managers reviewed the coming year's sales projections, production goals, and personnel plans and equipment needs. They disclosed when new products would hit the market and how big those markets were. They even delivered the tough news about plans to discontinue certain product lines or consolidate operations.

Discussing department head counts was "sensitive," chief financial officer Joe Hudetz admits, and a few employees worried about losing their jobs, but "you don't get many sour grapes when you're honest and tell them up-front." Fair warning allowed people to transfer or train for new positions in the company.

Once employees were given a glimpse of where the company was headed, they could concentrate on their own departments. During the afternoon of Brain Day, each department met to plan for the year. "It gave me a chance to think about the portion of the plan that involves me," says Sue Smith, a scheduling manager. "That way we could avoid some mistakes in advance."

According to Smith, prior warning about the company's European expansion plans allowed her department to install more timely and accurate shipping systems. "We'll have fewer weighing errors and delays shipping overseas," she says.

The payoff for the company? "Everything came in on target," Hudetz says. Sales increased 18%. Solar added almost 100 people and opened a new plant in Missouri. "With that kind of growth, there was no way we could have met the goals without everyone knowing what the game plan was."

44

Friendly Competition

Measuring up is no private affair at Environmental Compliance Services Inc. (ECS), in Exton, Pa. By posting the revenues produced in each department, CEO Bill Kronenberg III **opens up each profit center's performance to companywide scrutiny.**

Every month managers in six departments at the environmental insurance firm chart actual gross sales, compare them with the budget, then post the information on boards for all to see.

The result, says Kronenberg, is not only more competition but more cooperation among teams.

One year, when ECS's retail insurance unit hit a slump, several other departments—which had been tracking the downturn on Kronenberg's boards—came to the rescue. The underwriting group, ahead 40%, jumped in to provide new leads. Marketing helped make some cold calls. Thanks to the push, the retail shop came in 7% ahead in a flat market.

"It pays us dividends," Kronenberg says. "I don't have to watch as closely. I used to track the budget almost daily. Now I do it once weekly, and I don't even need to, really. They're watching those boards more closely than I ever would have expected."

"The real impediment
to productivity isn't the
workers, union or non-union;
it's management."

KEN IVERSON

CEO OF NUCOR CORP.

Turning Information into Profits

"We were managing a $5-million company with systems fit for a $1-million one," says Clay Page of the market downturn his company, Co-op Building Consultants, in Corpus Christi, Tex., faced in 1989. So Page **revamped the way his construction company tracks costs, schedules work, and trains employees.**

The results? In just one year employees have become 40% more productive, with only a 6% rise in costs. And Page's business has increased by 10%. His strategy included:

1. Tracking costs in small units. Page categorized construction tasks into 6,000 items (the average for his niche is 200), then entered them, along with the associated hourly costs for labor and materials, into a database. As a result, he can calculate more accurate project estimates.

The company also provides employees with flowcharts diagramming the order of tasks and how long each should take. Employees note and report deviations from their flowchart estimates.

2. Holding quarterly wrap-up meetings. Page spends one day each quarter with each of his six crews, sans supervisors, to discuss tasks that were 6% over or under budget. A supervisors' meeting, which Page does not attend, is also held. Beforehand, however, he does give supervisors a summary of his reactions to the past quarter's projects, including a list of problems to solve. Finally, at a 15-minute companywide meeting, information gleaned at each of the crew meetings is shared with everybody.

3. Sharing rewards with employees. Page pays employees hourly rates just below union rates and attaches a bonus to each project based on time and profitability targets. That usually brings his 36 employees' wages above the union rates. He also posts pay rates for different skills as an incentive for workers to build their expertise.

Employees have adapted to the new management system so well that Page has promoted from within for all supervisory positions. "This system isn't made for everyone," he says, "but it's perfect for the hard workers we want on our side."

Controlling Meeting Mania

There was a time at Eriez Magnetics when customers would call, and possibly six engineers would be tied up in a meeting unable to respond to the customers' inquiries. But no more. Matter of fact, you won't find *anyone* in the company in a meeting during business hours.

As part of a commitment to customer service, no staff meetings are allowed at the company between 9:00 A.M. and 4:30 P.M., so that everyone can be available to customers at all times. By 9:00 in the morning, all meetings for the day have been completed. If a meeting requires more time, it can begin again after 4:30 P.M.

Says Chet Giermak, CEO of this $55-million industrial-equipment manufacturer in Erie, Pa., "You'd be surprised how a policy like this cuts down on the number of unnecessary meetings and forces people to make decisions." There was grumbling when meeting black-out times were established years ago, but according to Giermak, the company soon got used to it. At Eriez, the workday runs from 8:00 A.M. to 4:30 P.M., with meetings beginning as early as they need to in order to be completed by 9:00. Hourly employees, who may have to stay for a post-4:30 or Saturday meeting, are paid overtime.

Have there ever been exceptions to the rule? If necessary, emergency stand-up meetings are allowed, as are meetings with outside visitors, but otherwise, no exceptions. At 9:10 A.M., if a meeting has run into overtime, Giermak himself has been known to walk in and help grease the skids for a speedy conclusion.

47

The All-Purpose Incentive System

"Four years ago our personnel roster was nearing the 50 mark, though we were grossing less than one-third of our current revenues. We were staffed with too many doing too little. Our energies and monies were spent on training new employees, only to lose others to any factory that hung up a shingle....Only revolutionary change could save us."

So wrote Carol Gordy, president of Natural Decorations Inc. (NDI), a maker of dried-flower and artificial-flower arrangements in Evergreen, Ala. After setting up performance bonus systems, Gordy got some good results, but was bothered by the piecemeal nature of the criteria. "Employees needed to be challenged and compensated for exceptional performance in all areas," she explains. She wanted to reward them for their daily achievements, not just in a competition with others.

She **devised a bonus system for productivity** (see below). Each employee starts with 50 points. Each month NDI's employees receive their personal calculation for the previous 30 days. If the employee ends up with a positive number, she receives a bonus check. Gordy made each bonus point worth $1. Some employees earned more than $1,000 in bonuses for the year, on a salary of about $12,500.

This plan has had a dramatic effect on the company. NDI's 33 employees are supporting revenues of $3.3 million, although it took nearly 50 people to produce $1 million worth four years ago. The bonus dollars awarded have increased almost every month because employees are taking less time off from work and reworks are at a minimum. Plus, NDI has not lost any designers in two years.

Automatic Initial Points...+50 Points

Tardiness...-5 x # of days =

Time off...-10 x # of days =

Absenteeism..-15 x # of days =

Reworks ....-5 x # of times =

Safety, maintenance,& procedural infractions ....-5 x # of times =

Production time above average ....+2 x # of days =

Production time below average ....-2 x # of days =_____

TOTAL =

You Get What You Pay For

Scott Davis, director of operations for Autodesk Inc., a Sausalito, Calif., software maker, was **buying time—not productivity—by paying his production workers hourly wages.** "People were working overtime who didn't need to, and the error rate was very high," he recalls. So he put his employees on salary and offered them a monthly productivity bonus—eliminating the incentive to work overtime. Six months out, errors had all but disappeared.

Five years ago, when Davis started the bonus system, he was managing 14 employees and the company had sales of $29 million. By 1990 sales had grown to $200 million, but his staff had grown only to 27. Today 90% of the production workers take home the bonus, which makes their pay 10% to 15% more than it would be if they still worked for an hourly wage.

War on Drugs

In 1980, suspected employee drug use was reported to Jack Longbine, employee resources director at Oregon Steel Mills Inc. (OSM) in Portland, Ore. He acted immediately, but it was the way he acted that was significant. Management edicts in this unionized company of 650 people usually did not sit well. So he went directly to the employees, setting up a 12-member **employee-assistance committee to set policies on dealing with drugs and alcohol in the workforce.** The agreement was that management could veto any of their ideas, but it could not implement anything that the committee did not recommend.

The committee's first action was to recognize drug addiction as an illness. No employee, except in such cases as theft, can be fired without first getting a chance at rehabilitation. The committee also set up a drug-education program.

Anyone who tests positive for drugs has three choices—immediate discharge, the opportunity to fight the findings through a conflict-management board, or signing a last-chance work agreement, which places the employee on two-year probation and requires random drug testing and enrollment in a mandatory drug treatment program. Failure to meet these requirements or maintain good work performance are grounds for dismissal.

The cost-benefit analysis has been hard to gauge. The drug-education program runs the company about $48 per employee in lost production time. The rehabilitation costs are handled through an HMO, with premiums increasing substantially each year. But then there's productivity. In 10 years, productivity has increased 140%. The accident rate has dropped by 60%, and the absentee rate has plummeted from 14 days to 1.5 days per year for employees who have received treatment. The drug program is probably one of a few factors contributing to this increase, helped by the fact that the company is now largely employee-owned.

Regardless of the uncertainties of cost-benefit statistics, Longbine feels there is no question that the program is paying off. "Any company that says it doesn't have a drug problem is just fooling itself," he says. "We have a lot fewer problems now. People are more willing to admit things and seek help."

Safety at All Costs

Enforcing safety rules can be a thankless job, unless the rules themselves become *self-enforcing*.

That's the principle Howard Kraye used to address the safety policies of his start-up business. At Cable Technology Corp. (CTC), a high-tech electronics company in Albuquerque, Kraye **set up a program that made it both fun and profitable for employees to constantly monitor themselves and others for safety violations.**

If any employee (or associate, as they are called) violates a safety rule—for example, not wearing safety glasses—any other associate can call him or her on it and the offender has to put a $1 fine into a monthly lottery. At the end of each month, everyone is given a lottery ticket, and a drawing is held to award the winning ticket with all the money collected in fines that month. The monthly pool normally averages from $70 to $100.

The response from associates has been so positive, the pool has been expanded to include other infractions, such as not filling out labor logs correctly or on time. The results of the program have been just as upbeat. Since the company's start-up a year ago, there have been no injuries, unless you count the time that one associate got a scissors cut. But if everyone is so careful, why doesn't the pool dry up? The company is growing fast enough—14 to 72 associates in the past year—that new associates' infractions continually fund the lottery. More senior associates account for only 3% of the fines on average.

Besides a good safety record, CTC received the U.S. Senate Productivity Award in 1991, tying with a company with a much longer track record, Intel Corp. Safety and productivity are top-of-the-mind concerns for everyone at CTC. As Kraye says, using one violation as an example, "No one, except the Pope, is exempt from wearing safety glasses when they enter the plant." But then again, they don't expect the Pope to visit any time soon.

The Custom-Made Day Planner

According to time-management experts, there's no *one* right way to manage time. Just as choosing what breakfast cereal you eat in the morning is a personal decision, so too is how you organize your time. But **developing a daily planning system that works for you can make you, and your company, more productive.**

Hyrum Smith, CEO of Franklin International Institute in Salt Lake City and developer of the Franklin Day Planner, is on one extreme of the time management spectrum. In his daily planner, he prioritizes tasks by rating them A through C, and then breaks these priorities down further with numbers. By doing this, he feels he can remain focused on long-term goals by dividing them into bite-size chunks. Smith's system also includes a group of status indicators that go beyond the simple check mark; for instance, task completed, task delegated, task in progress. By the end of each day, every task has been addressed in one form or another and Smith believes he is one step closer to completing long-term goals. Says Smith, "Rarely if ever are ad-hoc to-do lists created with an eye toward meeting long-term goals."

John Katzman, however, CEO of Princeton Review, a company based in New York City that prepares people to take the SATs, GREs, and LSATs, has little use for regimented planner systems. In his opinion, "you end up spending more time reorganizing the planner than taking action. An inefficient personality won't be any better off with a day planner than with a to-do list." Katzman's scrappy, little daily to-do list has all the information he needs to complete his day—phone numbers for all the calls required, meeting schedules, and tasks to be delegated. Not that daily decisions shouldn't be tethered to long-term goals, says Katzman, but there is no need to take overt steps to align the two. Those goals are the "categorical imperative behind every project I'm working on," he says.

Bar the Doors

Do you often find by the end of the day that you've spent all your time on other people's priorities and totally ignored your own? And that your to-do list, if you use one, looks just as it did that morning, except now it's longer?

Many people try to regain the time they've "given away" by arriving at the office an hour earlier before the phones ring and people start knocking at their door. But as often happens, people then learn your daily routine and you fall back into your old habits. All you have managed to do is extend your workday by an hour without sheltering any additional productive time for yourself.

Alex Baker, owner of Career Center, a placement agency in Needham, Mass., finally realized she just couldn't afford to give away her own time so freely to others. Who was the major culprit stealing Baker's time? "I was, definitely," admits Baker. "Both my employees and my clients were more likely to respect my time than I was." So **she decided to make unbreakable appointments with herself. This allowed her to protect certain times each day for her own important projects and priorities.** Everyone in the company was made aware of those times and avoided interruptions. Again, it proved to be most difficult for Baker. "It took some hard work on my part not to break appointments with myself," she says, "but I soon learned to value my commitment to high-priority projects of my own, as well as those of my staff."

Winning the Paper Chase

"I thought someone said we were working toward a paperless society with the advent of computers. Don't you believe it. We were drowning in paper. We had to do something," says Karen Lischick, one of the founders of Alexandria Aerodrome, a health and fitness company based in Alexandria, Va.

So the company **devised a two-step approach to paper management to ensure that things were done on schedule and that people weren't spending unproductive time** simply shifting papers from one side of their desk to the other.

Step one requires that every single piece of paper that survives the qualifying process when the mail is opened be given a projected life span. Then each person asks herself a series of questions, starting with, "Do *I* need to respond to this? (or can someone else? Or, does it need to be responded to at all?)" If the answer is yes, the second question is, "Will it take more than five minutes?" If yes again, the document is then given a date or time on the upper right-hand corner. By that date, the process must be completed or reevaluated and redated.

Step two requires that each dated page be filed in a "tickler file" composed of 43 labeled openings—for days 1 through 31 and months January through December. So, for example, at the beginning of each month, Lischick takes all her documents for that month and distributes them into the day files based on the date notations in the upper corners.

Now when Lischick arrives at work each morning, she just pulls out the documents for that day and takes action on them immediately. The paper monster hasn't been slain at Alexandria Aerodrome, but it has been tamed.

"Our problem in the
U.S. isn't overemphasis
on incentives;
it's that so few companies
offer them at all."

TOM PETERS

Penny-Pinching Ideas

When times are tough, the tough sometimes need a little help to get going. But spending cash on incentive awards may be the last thing you can afford. Here are **some creative, low-cost ideas for rewards:**

• The thanks-for-the-loan-of-your-spouse prize. Chris Carey, president of Datatec, a Fairfield, N.J., company that installs in-store computer systems, measures success through customer surveys. The employee with the highest quarterly survey score receives a plaque of recognition. And the employee's spouse receives a letter of appreciation and a certificate for a free dinner for two.

• Perfectionism has its rewards. Using the same customer surveys, Datatec also traces the number of perfect scores per job site on a monthly basis. Workers who raked in the greatest number of perfect scores receive a "data dollar," which can be used to purchase products from a catalog.

• Pampering without guilt. Happy Feet Day was born the afternoon that Linda L. Miles, president of Linda L. Miles & Associates, in Virginia Beach, Va., stole away from the office to have a pedicure. Miles, who with her mostly female staff designs and conducts seminars, thought it might be nice for everyone to take an hour off to get pedicures. Total tab: $175, plus tip.

• Monopoly money with purchasing power. When Pam Reynolds, president of Phoenix Textiles, a St. Louis health-care linen supplier, wanted to design a new incentive system, she invented a new currency: "bird bills." Employees could earn the play money through excellent performance in 10 to 15 areas. To foster teamwork every employee was also granted a "bank account" of bird bills, which could be given to other employees who helped them. At year-end Phoenix hosted a party and auction at which employees could use their bird bills to buy items such as movie tickets, a cruise, or a fax machine. The cost of about $15,000 (including dinner and the auction) may seem high, but the program's cost per person is only about $214.

READER'S CHOICE

55

A Lottery of Thanks

As Mae West would say (in another context, of course), "Too much of a good thing is wonderful." Well, John Adams, president of Adams & Adams Building Services Inc., feels the same way when it comes to rewarding his employees for a job well done.

Ever since the founding of his commercial janitorial service company in Enfield, Conn. 10 years ago, Adams has made a point of acknowledging good work among his now 200 employees (or "members," as they are called in the company). Over the years he has continually tried to improve his "pat-on-the-back" techniques, but one hurdle he faced was getting his supervisors as invested as he was in the practice. "I always like to say thanks," says Adams. "But a lot of our managers had a hard time saying thanks as readily. So I **needed a way to make it easier and quicker to acknowledge good work at the moment it occurs, not six months after the fact."**

To address these issues, Adams created the Instant Recognition and Awards Program (IRAP), which combines a recognition program with incentives. Supervisors are given a set of congratulatory notecards that are small enough to fit in their pockets. When a supervisor sees good work or an achievement among the members, this notecard is filled out with thanks for the particular effort and given to the member on the spot. These notes also double as tickets that are entered in a company lottery for prizes. There are three different levels of achievement that correspond to a certain number of chances in the lottery.

Twice a year the company holds a lottery drawing as part of their recognition gatherings. Members know exactly how many chances they have because they know how many thank-you tickets they have received over the past six months. Six tickets are drawn with prizes ranging from answering machines to VCRs to trips. The cost of the program for the company is less than $2,000 a year.

The program has received such high marks from both members and supervisors that Adams is now thinking about having monthly drawings of smaller amounts to make the thanks even more immediate.

In the Cards

Looking to decrease accidents and the number of days your employees call in sick? How about a nice game of cards? Scott Pilato and Andy Juster, cofounders of Sunny Waterbeds & Accessories, in Orlando, let **workers pick a card from a poker deck if they had perfect attendance and no time lost due to accidents** during the preceding five workdays.

After seven weeks the value of the cards is tallied (face cards count as 10 points). The two people with the highest and lowest total split the pot, which starts at $200 and increases by $100 for each seven-week period all 45 employees go without an accident.

"We started this a year ago after the state increased our workers' compensation by 29%, because of our high accident rate," says Pilato. "Basically, we take the money we were paying in medical bills and put it in the pot. But the program has been so effective that our workers' comp will be $2,000 less next year. Employees are more careful, and they remind each other to be more careful, so the size of the pot keeps increasing."

Overcoming the Aging Process

When collections slip, the last thing you want to do is give customers a reason *not* to pay you. "Unhappy customers tend to stretch their payments or not pay at all," says Craig Tysdal, vice-president of sales for Network Equipment Technologies. **To bolster customer service and get payments in the door, the company pays sales managers bonuses based on the age of accounts receivable.**

Twice a month, the Redwood City, Calif., company publishes a profile of receivables, broken down by region and district, that shows which accounts are current and which are 30, 60, or 90 days old or more. The bonus, paid quarterly, is determined by how well managers meet goals for each level of the aging schedule. The more the sales manager exceeds the goals for a particular level, the larger the bonus he receives. Tysdal reports that within a year after the bonus system was set up, the number of receivables that are more than 90 days old had been cut in half.

Getting Your Employees to Ask for More Work

John Dieball knew his customers wanted their computers fixed quickly. He also knew, since fixed monthly fees were charged for service, that fixing customers' computers quickly and correctly the first time, would allow his field staff to make more calls and add more profit. The customers would be happy, the company would be more profitable, but how do you convince the field staff?

Simple. Make it worth their while. Last year, Jadtec Computer Group in Orange, Calif., a computer repair company, **designed a program to incentivize the 10-person field staff to reduce costs.** The incentive system rewards points for such things as closing a call on the first visit and repairing a part, instead of replacing it. And on the down side, exacting penalty points if the service person has to be called back for further repairs. Besides points earned for successful service calls, the vice-president of operations can also award 25 special points on a discretionary basis each month for extraordinary work. A software program was developed and tied into the dispatching system to track the points earned so that results can be posted twice a month.

Quarterly, the points are totaled for each employee, and 3% of the company's profits for the period are then paid out based on the distribution of points in the pool. Payouts average from $200 up to $900 per employee every three months. As Dieball reports, "The program has been working like a bloody charm. We'll even get calls now at 3:00 in the afternoon from field staff looking for more work." Output increased 20% and profits did even better. Dieball expects that as the business grows, the members of his field staff are going to fight additional hires, taking on even more work themselves, rather than shrinking their own piece of the pie.

Instant Gratification

You may not be getting the most out of your profit-sharing plan if your employees have to wait until the end of the year to see their money. "If you can give the reward closer to the time of the action, then you'll stimulate the right response," says Bob Shaw, CEO of Allied Plywood Corp., in Alexandria, Va.

Shaw **doles out profit sharing on a monthly basis.** He claims it takes hardly any extra time to calculate—and that his 80-plus employees work harder, need less supervision, and are absent an average of only two days a year. "They police each other because they understand how the money gets into their pockets," he says.

"It's tough when profits fall," concedes Shaw, whose company's annual sales were just over $31 million last year. "It's a bit of a demotivator. Fortunately, employees also remember last month, when times were good."

The Element of Surprise

Dave Wiegand, president of Advanced Network Design Inc. (AND), a La Mirada, Calif., telecommunications company, used to get employees to do what he wanted by using an old stand-by—incentives. AND had weekly, monthly, and quarterly awards workers could earn. The carrots worked but with a hitch. "We'd start a program to motivate a certain behavior," he recalls. "When we stopped a program, we'd lose that behavior."

So in 1988 Wiegand **started a new award system: no system. Now his employees don't know who will get bonuses or what they will be.** "Out of the blue we'll call a meeting and reward somebody for outstanding performance," says Wiegand, who gave 15 awards worth some $9,000 at two meetings last year.

The size of the reward depends on the profitability of the activity being rewarded. Last year Wiegand gave a five-day family vacation to Disney World to one executive because his department's sales had exceeded expectations by 70%; a $75 clock radio to an unusually dependable receptionist; and a $375 suit to a manager (with pearl jewelry for his wife) who had increased his department's revenues 40% in four months.

Intermittent reinforcement, says Wiegand, is far more effective than defined bonus plans. Under the new system AND's sales force has shrunk from 12 to 4 while productivity has increased. Where the top salespeople had generated $110,000 in annual new revenues, the two top saleswomen brought in $638,000 and $520,000 in new revenues last year. Plus, the company isn't locked into the fixed cost of a traditional incentive program.

"Some people think
this is no way to run a company.
But the way I look at it,
I can't lose. The more money
they make, the more I make."

JERRY HUDSON

CEO OF HYDRA-TECH INC.

Raising the Bar for Bonuses

Bonuses should be wonderful things to give and to receive, but the classic year-end bonus—the one you get for making your budget numbers—often fails to motivate.

That's why Art Spinner, a founding general partner of Hambro International Venture Fund, is gravitating toward more objective bonus systems. At Tylan General, a $35-million instrumentation company in San Diego, he and other members of the executive committee have set up a new plan: the top four officers of the company must achieve 75% of their budgeted plan to get a bonus. Beyond that, the executives will receive a straight percentage of pretax net income.

Tylan CEO David Ferran's bonus, for example, is 6% of his pretax net income. Previously, he could get no more than 25% of his base pay in a year-end bonus, if the board decided he'd done a good job. "Now the sky's the limit," he says. This **new approach motivates managers to increase sales and cut costs.** Says Ferran: "If we find a way to save $1 million, that's 60 grand in my pocket. You'd better believe I'm looking for ways to save money."

On the Road Again

To minimize employee wear and tear, if an out-of-town job spills over from Friday to Monday for an Electronic Liquid Fillers Inc. employee, he gets **an extra week's pay for spending the weekend in the city of the job site.** CEO Jim Ake figures the expense is incidental when the payoff is having a refreshed employee on the job at 7:00 a.m. Monday morning.

Six to eight times a year each member of Ake's 33 bottling machine sales and installation staff spends weekends working away from the $11-million LaPorte, Ind., company. "Given the choice between flying back and forth or staying over, 9 times out of 10 they'll stay over," says Ake, who would just as soon see the money saved on the plane ticket—usually about a week's pay—go into the employee's pocket.

"They're on the road so much that it's not the kind of policy that's abused," says Ake. "But they do appreciate it."

Rethinking Quotas

In the beginning it made sense to pay your salespeople using a straight revenue-based quota system. After all, the goal was to sell, period. Now profits mean as much as or more than volume.

Rick Rose, president of Dataflex, has **devised a more balanced compensation plan that feeds corporate goals and enables him to more equitably rank the 13 salespeople** at the Edison, N.J., company, which resells and maintains PCs and peripherals.

Borrowing from Big Blue, Rose created a balanced performance quota (BPQ). "In any sales force, you have multiple things going on—maintaining old accounts, going after new business," Rose notes. For example, for a new account rep: hitting the goal of landing x new accounts is worth 40% toward quota; hitting y gross profit margin (sales minus cost of goods sold, divided by sales) is worth 40%; and bringing in z revenues, 20%. But for a territory rep (the next level up), the BPQ differs significantly: the gross-profit-margin goal is worth 50%, the revenue goal 25%, and the product-mix goal—selling a range of products and services—is 25%.

"When we do our sales goals each year, we make the BPQ the minimum requirement," Rose says. Dataflex's commission structure (all salespeople work only on commission) is based on reaching 100% of the BPQ. Most make it or exceed it, he reports. There's no cap. "The more they exceed their BPQ, the more they make." The payoffs of the BPQ are:

• Increased profit margin. Within three years Dataflex's gross profit margin rose from 15.4% to 17.2%. The emphasis on margin helps salespeople decide how to use their time.

• More profitable sales. To underline the importance of selling from the company's product mix—namely services—for the territory sales rep, product mix has the same weight as revenues. While Dataflex sells lots of hardware, "services are where we really make our margins."

• Motivated sales force. In three years sales have increased from $23 million to $93 million. "The corporate goal was 20% to 25% growth," Rose marvels. "That means a lot of salespeople did two to three times what was asked of them."

Pay for Performance Only

Chet Giermak, CEO of Eriez Magnetics, tells the story of a supervisor conducting salary reviews with two welders. One welder shows up for work on time every day, the quality of his work results in few rejects, and he cooperates well with his co-workers and his boss. The second welder sometimes arrives at work late, has more rejects, and has been known to have some problems with his co-workers. The punch line? They both get a 5% general increase for the year.

To Giermak, this makes no sense and is patently unfair. He has little use for general increases, having discontinued them five years ago. Now at Eriez, a $55-million industrial-equipment manufacturer in Erie, Pa., **all employees receive increases based on merit only.** Everyone is told the performance requirements to meet the salary guideline set for the year based on company results. Managers have the responsibility to determine whether people have performed up to the guideline, say 5%, or deserve more or less. If over the guideline, for example, 7%, the employee automatically gets the guideline 5% in his paycheck thereafter and receives the additional 2% in the form of a bonus check on the spot. In the case of substandard performance, a smaller-than-guideline percentage increase is given or none at all, with the understanding that if the employee improves in the six months to follow, that percentage can be adjusted upward.

The merit policy has worked well for the company, with the added benefit of making Eriez's managers *better* managers. "With only a general increase," says Giermak, " managers really don't have to manage."

When it comes to performance, Giermak and Eriez are committed to doing everything they can to support and generously reward employees. But if the issue is simply wanting more money to match inflation, regardless of performance, "they'll have to go see their congressman," says Giermak.

Freshening Up

Have you ever seen a **sales force view commissions more as Social Security checks than as a reason to drum up new business?** Rick Johnson has. So when he founded BurJon Steel Service Center Inc., in Springboro, Ohio, he made some changes.

Tired of seeing some salespeople live off old accounts, he decided to eliminate commissions on accounts once they have been with BurJon for one year. The client becomes a house account, still serviced by the original rep, but money goes into companywide profit sharing instead of into commissions.

Johnson reads weekly call reports to ensure that house accounts remain well cared for. Though commissions cease, reps who do good work with old clients can receive year-end bonuses—of as much as $10,000—and salary adjustments.

The big money, though, is in new customers, Johnson says. "There is unlimited commission potential here, but you've got to write new business to exploit it."

Overall, the system seems to have worked. The company's revenues have risen from $1 million to $20 million in seven years.

A Globetrotting Guide to Compensation

When it comes to compensation traditions around the world, the old saying—different strokes for different folks—definitely applies.

Some of the knottiest problems that companies face when they open a foreign office are managing within the country norms. Compensation expectations will differ, as will motivational techniques and bonus disbursement. Local workers may embrace performance bonuses in one country, or shrug their shoulders at them in another. Here are **general salary and bonus guidelines for five different countries** gathered from owners of U.S. companies who have ventured abroad:

GREAT BRITAIN:

It's difficult to find people to work for straight commission. A Christmas bonus is expected by everyone. High tax rates make objects rather than cash a preferable motivator. Cost of a good electronic engineer: $25,000.

HUNGARY:

High tax rates make bonuses not very rewarding, so they aren't expected. Travel abroad is prized. Cost of a good electronic engineer: $10,000.

JAPAN:

Bonuses for individual performance are unpopular. Employees prefer straight salary. All receive New Year's bonus based on company's performance: 1.2 times a month's salary in a good year, half a month's salary in a bad year. Cost of a good electronic engineer: $30,000.

SOUTH KOREA:

Employees respond well to commission only. Spring, fall and New Year's bonuses are expected; size of bonuses reflects company performance. Cost of a good engineer: $19,000

BELGIUM:

Almost every employee participates in a bonus plan. Employees also get a separate bonus (called a "holiday package"), equal to 3 weeks salary, when they take their vacation. Cost of a good electronic engineer: $35,000.

Commissions That Smooth Out Sales

Like a lot of companies that rely on a field sales force, Software 2000 Inc., a computer-software developer in Hyannis, Mass., motivated their people by raising the commission rates on sales exceeding quota. So the incentive was to close as many sales as possible before the end of the year, while the salesperson could still earn the highest commission rate. The result: fully half of the company's sales closed during the company's last fiscal quarter. But with every sale came a demand to service the new customer.

To smooth out the company's sales and production load, president Doug MacIntyre revised the system. Now the commission-rate multiplier changes monthly in proportion to the rep's performance—total actual divided by total quota—over the previous six months. That means that the sales rep's performance *this* month will affect *future* commission rates, but the current month's rate is strictly a function of past performance.

The purpose of this "rolling quota" compensation plan is to keep sales at or above quota every month. The result is a smoother, more predictable revenue flow and the ability to better predict the need for customer-support services.

Why a *six*-month rolling quota? According to Atlanta consultant Warren Culpepper, who helped Software 2000 design its system, the length of the period depends in part on the length of the company's typical sales cycle. If closing a sale normally takes 90 days, you want the period of your rolling quota to be longer than that. But if you make the rolling-quota period too long, salespeople will find it difficult to affect their commission-rate multipliers in a reasonable length of time.

When kicking off a rolling-quota plan, you must start everyone out with an assumed past performance. Start with numbers somewhat lower than you actually expect. That way, in the early months of the new system salespeople have only to hit their quotas to kick their commission rates up a little. They'll come to like the new plan sooner.

Lastly, don't include the current month in the rolling average. That allows a rep to affect the rate paid on *this* month's sales, precisely what you're trying to avoid.

"I like creating the opportunity for people to have economic independence...which means building equity. Salary I always considered to be something you spend. Equity is something you build."

STEVE BOSTIC

CEO OF R. STEVENS CORP.

Profit Sharing that Works

Many CEOs fear that formalizing a profit-sharing arrangement with employees would rob their businesses of capital and, ultimately, stunt growth. But to Richard Dapson, president of Anatech, a supplier of chemicals to hospitals, profit sharing is the fuel behind his Battle Creek, Mich., company's 25% yearly growth rate.

At Anatech, profit sharing takes two forms: cash bonuses, which range from .75% to 2.0% of pretax profits, whenever there is a profit; and retirement-savings contributions equal to 10% of each person's wages plus bonus, paid by the company into a simplified employee pension (SEP) plan. Below, some tips from Dapson on **how to tailor profit-sharing plans to motivate employees:**

• Make frequent contributions. Anatech pays its bonuses and SEP contributions monthly. "Because the rewards are tied to current performance, people keep track of sales each day, so they can see if they'll get those bonuses," Dapson says.

• Keep plans simple. One priority of Dapson's was to make the connection between corporate results and individual rewards simple enough for everyone to understand. "I wanted people to be able to calculate while they're doing their jobs that if sales go up by x, their next bonuses will add up to y," he says.

• Don't attach strings. Because he felt confident about having designed an attractive compensation scheme, Dapson didn't set up a prolonged vesting schedule to tie employees to the company.

• Be fair. At Anatech, even part-time workers participate in the profit-sharing plans once they've worked for the company for several months. Fair sharing is so ingrained that when Dapson and his two partners reward themselves with extra bonuses, they write extra profit-sharing checks for their employees as well.

Building a Successful 401(k)

For the growing number of small companies starting 401(k)s, careful follow-up attention is every bit as important as good plan design. That's because companies that fail to aggressively recruit and retain 401(k) participants may run afoul of IRS regulations against "top-heavy" executive-skewed plans—and thus, risk losing tax benefits for employees.

Here's how Aerodyne Controls, a Ronkonkoma, N.Y., manufacturer of aerospace products with 75 employees, has **succeeded in attracting widespread participation for its 10-year-old 401(k) plan:**

• Personalized updates. "We used to send participants a report once a year on how much their accounts contained and how much they were earning in interest, but then decided the information was so positive, we should circulate it every six months," explains Robert Tripodi, one of Aerodyne's owners. Participants are frequently surprised by how much their accounts contain, since the company matches 50% of each employee's income-tax-free contribution.

• Extended vesting schedules. Employees are encouraged to remain in the plan by a vesting schedule that kicks in slowly: they are vested 25% after three years, and 100% only after five years.

• Follow-up interviews from top management. When employees ask to pull out of the 401(k), Tripodi meets with them. "I tell them they're missing out on saving money on taxes and preparing for retirement," he says. "I show them the financial costs and benefits so clearly that they can see the benefits of perhaps *reducing* their contribution, but the great costs of withdrawing entirely." That coincides with Aerodyne's interests, since withdrawals, not contribution reductions, run the risk of causing IRS problems.

Hassle-free Long-term Rewards

Performance unit plans (PUPs) make good sense for small businesses. **Unlike year-end bonuses, PUPs tie financial rewards to long-term, individual achievements, yet they don't entail prolonged financial obligations the way many phantom-stock or profit-sharing plans do.** Here's how they work:

1. A company's owner (or benefits specialist) selects the goal that makes sense for each executive. For example, a sales manager's target might be increased revenues, whereas a quality-control officer's might be reduced product rejects.

2. Owners attach to the goal specific numbers, which generally take the form of targeted percentages of change. Those percentages usually are stretched out over a three- to five-year horizon.

3. Then a PUP document is drawn up. In it, the executive is given a number of performance units, which have no value when they are issued. A clause states that if the executive achieves his or her PUP goals over a defined period, each unit will increase in value to the point where it can be redeemed for its new value, in effect as a cash reward.

"Growth-oriented companies can set executives' goals really high but then include a prorated reward structure so that managers who don't quite make it won't get burned out and leave," says Adam Gaslowitz, an Atlanta lawyer who has helped small companies design PUPs. Companies can also keep setting up new PUP plans for key executives, with revised goals that make sense for the company in its latest growth phase. So if executives are always in the midst of earning new performance units—which they know they'll lose if they resign before the PUP matures—there's a real inducement to stay with the business.

The Time-honored ESOP Buyout

Employee stock ownership plans (ESOPs) continue to be a simple way to transfer ownership of private companies. They offer great tax advantages both to companies that use them and to banks that help finance them. When those breaks are combined with benefits from insurance policies, much of the cost of ESOP transactions can be offset.

Here's how the strategy works. The company owner sets up an ESOP in much the same way any benefits plan is established. Then the ESOP obtains bank financing to pay for the company stock the owner plans to sell to it. "Banks pay tax on only a portion of the interest paid to them by ESOPs, so they have an incentive to make these loans," says Richard Snipes, a benefits and insurance consultant at Barry, Evans, Josephs & Snipes Inc., in Charlotte, N.C.

The company, not its employees, then pays off the ESOP loan out of cash flow, by making contributions to the ESOP. That way, both the principal and the interest are tax deductible.

"The owner gets to sell off his stock at whatever annual pace appeals to him. There's no cost to the employees, who eventually get to take over the company. And for the company, the cost of the buyout is fully deductible," says Snipes.

There's only one big expense: the cost of buying out each employee, as is required by the IRS, upon the employee's departure. Normally, that's a burden the corporation has to bear, but Snipes suggests using company-owned life-insurance policies to provide the cash necessary when ESOP buyouts come due. "Companies can design policies so they will be financially cushioned, either through death benefits or by borrowing against the cash value that has accumulated in policies."

Are You Ready for Profit Sharing?

Many companies hesitate to set up profit-sharing plans for fear of the cost of upkeep or excessive regulations. Ed Lentz, secretary/treasurer of Lentz Milling Co., in Reading, Pa., dismisses those worries. "We pay a relatively small sum each year to reap the benefits of a satisfied work force," says Lentz.

To find out if you're ready to commit to a profit-sharing plan for your company, ask yourself these four questions:

• Does management see a need for either a company-wide retirement benefit or a tax shelter for owners? Profit-sharing plans can accomplish either objective, thanks to the fair degree of latitude companies have over plan design and distribution formulas. Lentz Milling distributes the maximum legally deductible amount to all 50 employees of the plan. But the IRS also allows highly paid workers, who are required to make larger Social Security contributions, to be rewarded at higher levels during profit-sharing time.

• Does the business generate enough cash flow to support a savings plan? "There's no point considering a profit-sharing plan if the company isn't already able to fund its business operations and growth plans, as well as more essential benefits like health or life insurance," says William Belanger, a benefits consultant at Noble Lowndes.

• Can management tolerate a long-term relationship with a consulting firm? IRS and Department of Labor regulations are so complicated that it's wise to use consultants or lawyers in plan design and drafting key documents. Expect to pay $2,500-$7,500 in setup costs, and another $1,000 or so each year to a consultant who will monitor regulatory changes and prepare employee updates and tax forms.

• Does management prefer a flexible arrangement over a commitment to mandatory annual contributions? Profit-sharing plans permit a high degree of flexibility when it comes to determining how much, if anything, is to be contributed each year by the employer. IRS rules allow no more than, basically, 15% of a company's total payroll to be deducted annually. "We emphasize to employees that there's no obligation at all for us to make any contributions if times get hard," says Lentz.

The ABCs of Phantom Stock

William Reidy, CEO of $8.2-million Fine Organics Corp., a chemical manufacturer in Lodi, N.J., had a problem: "We were buying two companies and **wanted to figure out how to retain key personnel,** but giving them stock shares in Fine Organics wasn't an option for us. Then we heard about phantom stock," recalls Reidy.

The basic scheme was simple: "Instead of real stock, we'd give these key individuals a document that, at the time it is issued, has a value of zero. As the book value of the combined equity—that is, Fine Organics and the acquired company—increases, the amount of that increased value is added to the original zero value of the phantom stock." At an agreed-upon point, the individual cashes in the phantom stock for the difference between its current and original value.

Reidy provides these guidelines:

• Keep the financial terms simple. "These plans can turn into nightmares if you have to keep calculating present values and inflation indexes," Reidy says. "We just pegged everything to the book value of our stock, which is easy to calculate and understand."

• Present the plan as a win-win benefit. Prepare a brochure that spells out key advantages. One plus, for example: unlike regular stock shares, there's no tax bill due when the employee receives phantom shares, since the IRS considers them a form of deferred compensation, taxable only when shares are cashed in.

• Offer plenty of cash-in options. One of the best things about phantom stock is that it gives employers the flexibility to design a stock benefit that fits individual employees' needs. "They can receive profits outright in the form of a cash bonus or receive the cash over a deferred-payment schedule that makes sense for them," Reidy explains.

• Tailor vesting schedules to the individual. Rather than settling upon one specified vesting schedule, Reidy negotiates each person's vesting individually. "That way you can take into account factors like a person's age and how much value you expect him or her to bring to the company over time." At Fine Organics, vesting periods of 5 and 10 years have been used.

The Executive-Compensation Strategist

There are plenty of **cost-effective ways to keep executives loyal and productive over the long term.** Besides options such as 401(k) plans and phantom stock, here are some others you might want to consider:

• Restricted stock awards. If your executives want to own stock, this is a way to minimize your company's risks. Restricted stock awards come with plenty of strings attached. Executives gain full ownership after a vesting period and can sell their shares back to the company only at specified intervals.

• Incentive stock options. Under the right conditions—such as in a company that plans to go public—ISOs are a good incentive. They give executives the right to buy stock at a discounted price at some specified future date. The executives expect that ultimately they will be able to sell their shares at a profit.

• Secular trusts. A secular trust provides one way to hold payments in a deferred-compensation plan. Companies can use secular trusts to set aside large sums for their executives' future needs and ideally tie executives to them over the long term. The trusts provide companies with an immediate tax deduction, but executives must pay current taxes on the money that goes into the trusts, which is certainly a disadvantage from their standpoint. But for people working for cash-strapped businesses, there's an advantage: since secular trust funds are segregated from working capital, employees' deferred compensation is secure.

• Rabbi trusts. If your company doesn't need an immediate tax deduction, these provide a vehicle for setting deferred-compensation funds aside so executives pay taxes only when funds are distributed—at which point the company finally gets to record its tax deduction.

Age-weighted Profit-sharing Plans

At Butler Rogers Baskett, a New York architectural firm, the owners face a fairly typical problem. "With only a couple of exceptions, we're a good bit older than most of our employees," explains Jonathan Butler, a principal at the firm.

"Since we have fewer years until our retirement, we want to be able to set aside in our retirement plan larger sums for the older owners than we would for the rest of the staff."

Until recently, that wasn't an option. The IRS required all "qualified"—that is, tax-sheltered—retirement plans to meet strict antidiscrimination tests. But now there's an alternative: age-weighted profit-sharing plans. "It's a revolutionary change," says David J. McKeon, a vice-president at the New England, a Boston insurance company that administers the plans. "The IRS will now allow companies to prove nondiscrimination if they can demonstrate that all employees will wind up with the same total benefits by the time they retire."

How much more should older employees receive? McKeon offers the following example: "Let's say you've got a firm with two employees: a 55-year-old owner who earns $200,000 and a 35-year-old employee earning $100,000. In a traditional plan, the owner would be limited to receiving two-thirds of any profits distributed to the plan, because his compensation amounted to two-thirds of the overall payroll. But once you work your way through the IRS's actuarial assumptions with age-weighted plans, and take into account that the 35-year-old will have 20 extra years to earn tax-free interest on this year's disbursement, you would wind up with a plan in which the owner could now receive about 90% of distributed profits."

With age-weighted plans, contribution levels should be recalculated each year as employees age. "But that's no big hassle," says Butler, who also does not anticipate any costs or complications in switching from an old-style plan. As of now, all new or redesigned plans to be based on the age-weighted concept will have to file IRS Form 5300 plan descriptions, which may result in about $1000 in consultant fees. "It's worth it," says Butler, "if the new plans allow us to leverage the interests of our principal owners."

"By providing [part-timers] with insurance, we've helped bring turnover to below 50% in an industry where it typically runs more than 100% annually. Thanks to lower turnover, we've saved more in training costs than we've spent on insurance."

HOWARD SCHULTZ

CEO OF STARBUCKS COFFEE CO.

A Cafeteria Plan
for the Little Guy

For many small companies, a cafeteria plan for benefits is often considered impractical—too much time and money to administer or too few employees to make it worthwhile. One CEO disregarded those hesitations and came up with his own scaled-down variation of a cafeteria plan—more like a "vending machine" model—to address the needs of his employees and the company.

John Dieball, president of Jadtec Computer Group, a $4-million computer sales and service company in Orange, Calif., set out to solve two problems at once. The first was skyrocketing health insurance costs, a portion of which he knew he would have to pass on to his employees. The second issue was the diverse nature of his 30-employee workforce. Everyone had different needs with respect to vacations, sick days, and group insurance.

In order to give everyone a choice, Dieball **set up a benefit pool for each employee.** Every month, the company credits the pool with $100 to $200, the amount depending on whether the employee is hourly, salaried, or management. In addition, each employee gets 15 hours a month, at his current hourly rate, credited to his pool for the first five years of service, 20 hours thereafter.

Employees can use this money however they please. A parent may want to pay for dependent coverage or a single person might want more days off. If someone is sick he can use his vacation days or vice versa. At the end of each month, all employees receive an account balance of the money available to them. Ultimately, if someone leaves the company, he gets his balance in cash upon departure.

According to Dieball, it has been a win-win proposition. For one, employees can now decide for themselves how to address their own needs. As for the company, it has been able to pass on some of the group health costs fairly to the employees. And lastly, the controller doesn't have as many headaches negotiating days off and sick days. The monthly statements tell it all, not to mention serving as a constant reminder to employees of the benefits they receive.

Dry Shoulder for Hire

Here's the deal: you can **pay someone else to handle your employees' personal problems.** Instead of confiding in you, your employee calls an independent counselor about any kind of problem—from drug abuse to a bad case of the blues. The counselor makes a diagnosis and guides the caller to treatment.

This hands-off approach is known as an employee-assistance program (EAP). The pitch goes like this: a dollar invested in an EAP is supposed to save $2 to $3 in reduced medical claims, absenteeism, and other productivity zappers. Perhaps the most persuasive argument for EAPs are these statistics: alcoholics are involved in 40% of industrial accidents; substance abusers' productivity is 25% to 33% lower than average; nonalcoholic members of an alcoholic's family use 10 times the number of sick days as do employees who don't have an alcoholic family member.

Ron Parks, president of Millard Manufacturing, a $5-million metal fabricator in Omaha, counts his EAP as a double time savings. Not only are troubled employees more quickly freed to concentrate on their jobs, but their supervisors don't have to spend as much time trying to solve a problem they don't really understand.

If you decide to purchase an EAP (the annual cost for an EAP is likely to be $35 to $40 for each employee family), look for the following traits:

• Independence. Beware of low-cost or no-cost EAPs that function as "feeders" for an alcoholic-treatment center, for example. Affiliations with hospitals or other institutions are OK if the EAP can prove it exercises independent judgment in referring clients.

• Financial stability. There are plenty of EAPs run by people without business experience. Ask to see the profit-and-loss statement. Request an explanation of management's business controls and plans for handling growth.

• Qualifications. Look for minimum qualifications of three to five years of post-master's-degree experience. Certified employee-assistance professionals (CEAPs) will have at least three years of experience. Counselors fielding calls must be highly trained to recognize a broad range of problems, particularly alcohol and drug dependency.

Making Employee Contributions Less Painful

With no end in sight to health-care cost inflation, many companies have concluded that there's no way to avoid some type of cost-shifting—usually to employees who must pay higher deductibles and a larger percentage of nonreimbursed expenses. And that can wreak havoc on employee morale.

Knox Semiconductor Inc., a Rockport, Maine manufacturer with 40 employees, opted for a more constructive approach: **at the same time the company introduced insurance-cost-control measures, it began providing each employee life insurance, a mutual-fund savings account, and short-term and long-term disability coverage.** And because of the unusual way the company financed these benefits, it wound up ahead in overall cost savings.

When John Morey, president of Knox Semiconductor, sat down to look at his insurance coverage in 1989, it was costing him $80,000 a year and was projected to cost $170,000 by 1991. So with his insurance broker, he came up with cost-saving measures, which included partially self-insuring medical benefits, and a higher deductible for employees. Savings kicked in immediately. In 1990 the price of coverage stabilized at $80,000, and in 1991 it was $110,000.

To simultaneously finance the new benefits, Knox started contributing $6 per employee weekly into a mutual fund administered by the insurance company. Employees must contribute $6 as well, which is deducted from after-tax weekly salaries. "Of that $12, we use $5 to buy each employee a whole-life insurance policy," says Morey. The longer an employee works for Knox, the larger that death benefit will grow. Employees that leave the company take the policy with them.

The rest of the joint weekly contribution stays in the employee's mutual fund until he removes it to pay off his deductibles, nonreimbursed medical charges, or other personal expenses. If employees decide to empty their accounts, they have to pay off, on their own, any medical bills the company doesn't cover.

The company has saved so much money through the new system, mainly thanks to its switch to partial self-insurance, that it can still afford to reimburse 80% of most workers' medical expenses.

Playing Hooky Doesn't Pay

The way most companies set up sick-day policies, there's an incentive for people to take the days, regardless of whether they need them. But Stan Torstenson, founder and CEO of Stan's Lumber Inc., a $20-million building-supply company in Twin Lakes, Wis., rewards his 85 employees for coming to work, provided they can. How? **By paying them cash for any of the three paid sick days they don't use.**

With lower absenteeism, Torstenson's three stores run more smoothly, he says. "When you have to shift someone from one area of the business to another," he notes, "you don't get the same job done."

Affordable Wellness Programs

The ounce-of-prevention approach to containing health-insurance costs has always seemed like a luxury that only well-healed companies could afford. Exercise rooms, running tracks, and locker rooms are almost non-existent among small companies. Yet it's those companies that stand to gain the most from promoting healthy habits. Only one big medical claim can wreak havoc on a small company's premium structure.

The bitter irony is that a wellness program doesn't have to be costly. Gene Bedient, owner of Bedient Pipe Organ Co. in Lincoln, Neb. created his own. He'd always believed in regular exercise and good eating habits. But not all of his 12 employees did.

Drawing on his own thoughts, he **wrote a booklet on staying well for his employees. He concluded the treatise with an incentive program:** he pays employees for every healthy task that they execute each month. For example, if you exercised three times a week during the month, that's worth $7. If you did not smoke, you collect $3. A real angel could collect more than $300 a year. Furthermore, workers who have perfect attendance throughout the year receive an extra $300.

After 10 months, there have been notable achievements, such as large weight loss by some employees. Bedient is currently paying out two-thirds of the amount achievable if all employees were model health citizens. Total cost to date: $2,300. Bedient's employees have been eager participants, in part because the company also joined a community wellness council that provides assessment and educational services for only $50 a year.

The payoff will be hard to assess for two or three years. Large companies, which have more experience with wellness programs, report powerful results. In 1989 the Scoular Grain Co. in Omaha, for example, saved $1,500 per employee in total health care costs as a result of a program. But Bedient himself isn't impatient about reaping such benefits. "In the long range, it will pay off. If your approach is simply that it's going to save you a lot of money, employees will sense that and be skeptical," he warns.

Reining in Workers' Comp Costs

Workers' compensation costs can be a heavy burden for any manufacturing company. At Preferred, a $7.7-million industrial roofing and painting contractor based in Fort Wayne, Ind., they've become of astronomical importance. At $300,000 yearly, workers' comp fees amount to nearly one-sixth of the company's total $1.9-million operating budget.

For CEO Craig Hartman, controlling workers' comp costs is a management priority. One of Preferred's **most effective cost-control strategies to date: self-insuring, through which the company pays all claims of $250 or less.**

Since in Indiana, state-mandated workers' comp fees are pegged to the *number* as well as the size of claims, simply decreasing filing frequency should cut Preferred's annual fees by about 10%, chief financial officer Lisa Roberts estimates—a savings far outweighing the expense of paying minor bills. Of course, there's plenty of room for maneuvering: the $250 cap can be raised or lowered at any point if Roberts and Hartman feel it's either too costly or too low to reduce filings.

With an expensive history of fraudulent claims by some employees, Preferred has also put law firms on retainer in Cleveland, where the company operates one of its contracting facilities, to investigate and possibly litigate every significant workers' comp claim of a suspicious nature.

The company has also begun to investigate the medical and employment backgrounds of potential hires, to screen out fraudulent claims before they happen. "Now that we're taking an aggressive stance," Hartman says, "we believe we'll eventually be able to reduce operating costs by 10% through our workers' comp savings alone."

Day Care
for All Ages

Maybe Stride Rite can't spell right, but it sure does set the pace for community responsibility. The Cambridge, Mass., shoe manufacturer pioneered on-site day-care centers for youngsters, 20 years ago. And in 1990, Stride Rite set up business's first **employer-supported day-care center to serve *oldsters.***

At a cost of some $800,000, Stride Rite gutted 8,500 square feet of corporate-office space and converted it into classrooms and activity areas containing both elder- and child-size furniture.

Workers with family members in day care contribute to the center on a sliding scale, which is pegged to household income. To bridge the gap, the Stride Rite Charitable Foundation contributes capital to the operating budget, and the company itself supplies in-kind support such as bookkeeping, administrative and legal services. Liability insurance is tacked onto the corporation's own policy.

"Worker loyalty to the company is tremendous," asserts director of Stride Rite Work/Family Programs Karen Leibold, who sees ranks of siblings from the same families in attendance year after year, indicating that a large number of employees are staying on the job.

On-site day care is no longer the province of larger corporations, Leibold believes; even companies with few employees can establish a center, tapping intergenerational neighbors to fill it. Indeed, Stride Rite's own facility is only half filled by employee kin; the remainder—young and old—come from the community at large.

A Globetrotting Guide to Benefits

Few U.S. companies are prepared for how different foreign workplace benefits can be from U.S. norms—and from one country to another. Benefits offered are typically a blend of what's legally required and what's voluntary. Here are **benefit highlights in four different countries** gathered from owners of U.S. companies:

GREAT BRITAIN: Private medical insurance to complement national health care. Pension plans not as common as in the U.S. Managers and salespeople expect company cars, often with phones. High tax rates have made objects, rather than cash, preferable to employees. Vacations run 3 to 5 weeks typically, but are not mandated by law. 8 legal holidays, but most companies offer 12.

HUNGARY: Health-care coverage is legally required and costs up to 40% of wages. But wage rates are low. Many companies make home-construction loans and provide lunch, commuting, and day-care allowances. There's a heavy penalty for trying to reduce benefits to employees. Company car. Pay in hard currency. Travel abroad is prized. 15 vacation days are required by law; companies typically add 1 to 9 days for every three years of service. 8 legal holidays.

JAPAN: National health-care and social-security costs are split 50/50 by employer and employee. Company must pay worker's comp and unemployment insurance, and pension costs. Transportation and lunch allowances. Expense budgets can run very high; a middle manager might entertain clients 5 nights a week. Company car for executives. Add chauffeur for top management. 2 weeks of vacation are required by law; often taken a day at a time. 20 legal holidays.

SOUTH KOREA: Companies with more than 10 employees must pay for one medical exam each year and set aside one month's salary per year, per employee, as severance. Many companies offer low or no-interest car and housing loans; Pick-up by car pool, graduating to company car and driver. For vice-presidents, a golf club membership and lessons. For salespeople, a generous lump-sum expense account, which employee may keep if he or she does not spend it all. Law requires three vacation days. 19 national holidays.

"When you know a guy has incredible talent but you can't harness it, you can't focus it, you can't get it into the system—it kills you."

JACK STACK

CEO OF SPRINGFIELD REMANUFACTURING CORP.

Assessing Your Associates

As part of a bottom-to-top revamping of its corporate structure and philosophy, YSI, a $28-million instrumentation maker in Yellow Springs, Ohio, instituted semiannual peer reviews in all work centers in its production area. The appraisals are the most important feedback an employee gets. Supervisors, or team leaders, may be asked to grade an individual, too, but their input holds no more weight than any other team member's.

Still, it's hard to rub elbows all day long with someone you've just criticized. Here are **some tips on how to make peer appraisals work:**

• Construct logical peer groups. Whether or not your company is organized around teams, take care that every member of a group relies on the other members to achieve a goal. A colleague's appraisal won't be meaningful if she doesn't care how well another member of the group does his job.

• Encourage interchangeable jobs. Employees at YSI cross-train themselves to be able to handle any one of several jobs a team must execute and are therefore better able to evaluate others' work.

• Go slow. Workers who are used to top-down appraisals mistrust this kind of initiative. One step to take in preparation for peer reviews: first introduce group appraisals to get people to compare their work with others' performance.

• Give workers the tools to succeed. YSI has applied liberal doses of training in interpersonal skills and problem solving to acclimate production workers to their new duties. The goal is for peer appraisal to become a continual process.

• Let workers control the consequences. Give teams the power to hire and fire. Morale plunged in a work center when it became clear that one of the hires was not working out. After taking every step possible to help the member improve, the team knew they couldn't tolerate her performance or pass the buck to another part of the company.

• Know when to give up. Not everyone is going to adjust to self-management. For months one work center focused so much energy on a member who was uncomfortable about not being told what to do. The only solution was to get the team member a new job in a more structured part of the company.

So How Am I Doing?

"**M**illions of people who run companies know they should be conducting annual employee appraisals, but they're not doing it," asserts Roger Flax, president of Motivational Systems, a West Orange, N.J., management- and sales-training company. "There's a lot of assuming that in small companies people are motivated, so there's not a lot of formal motivating," he says.

One answer may be the **employee-initiated appraisal, in which employees are told they can ask for a review from their manager.**

The on-demand appraisal isn't meant to replace a conventional semiannual review, but it promotes an attitude of self-management among workers and often makes critiques more honest. Edward Silverman, president of SOS Security Inc., a Parsippany, N.J., security-guard company with $25 million in sales, says the employee-initiated appraisal "encourages an open-door policy" at his company.

Flax suggests employees ask for as many reviews as they feel they need. Here are the seven questions he instructs employees to ask in their self-initiated appraisals:

1. Can you rate my performance from one to 10?
2. What do you feel are the strongest elements of my work?
3. What are the weakest elements?
4. Why didn't I get a 10 (highest rating)?
5. Where do you think I can go in my job or career in the next 18 months to four years?
6. What skills, training, or education do I need to get to that point?
7. What specifically can we agree on that I can do, beginning tomorrow?

Developing and Tracking Talent

At Granite Rock Co., in Watsonville, Calif., you won't find equity ownership or fancy incentive-compensation plans to keep people committed. But the company does have two benefits that work just as well, if not better—providing training (and a lot of it) and giving each employee the opportunity to move around and up in the company.

These benefits are institutionalized in **the company's novel approach to performance evaluations, a system it calls its Individual Professional Development Plan (IPDP).** Every year a worker sits down with his or her supervisor and maps out a series of goals—for skill development, training, advancement, and on-the-job accomplishments. A concrete-plant operator's list might include, "Know how to develop and implement an improved maintenance plan for the plant; gain knowledge of basic concrete-sales techniques." The IPDP includes a how-I'll-get-there section ("attend a seminar on maintenance requirements and maintenance tracking; spend approximately eight hours per quarter working with sales manager to learn basic selling techniques"), along with target dates. Every quarter, employees review their progress toward the goals.

The IPDP system offers practical benefits for the company: managers say it helps them spot talent and ambition that might otherwise be frittered away. Less tangibly, it helps build loyalty.

The cost of all the training, without which the IPDP could not exist, is substantial for Granite Rock—$1,000 per employee, or roughly $400,000 a year. But when you consider that some consultants estimate that the average cost of poor quality (redoing jobs, refunding money, losing customers) can run as high as 30% of sales, this would translate into an annual bill of $9 million for Granite Rock. More to the point, says CEO Bruce Woolpert, is the fact that sales and productivity continue to increase yearly, with the company remaining in the black through the recession without having to resort to price cuts as seen elsewhere in the industry.

87

Bugging the Phones

Bill Grimes, president of Travel Design, a start-up in Wyoming, Mich., had wanted to be less of an FBI agent and more of a coach to the 110 sales agents who worked for him at the Endless Vacation, a travel company he sold in 1990. So he allowed them to **record their conversations with customers. Then, at the employees' initiative, those recordings were reviewed by the employee and a supervisor.**

"About 25% of the agents took an interest in improving themselves," says Grimes, who plans to install the system at Travel Design. Letting employees monitor themselves, combined with a new training program, helped the company's commissions (earned per hour) rise by about 35%.

Tyler Phillips is also instituting self-taping, for different reasons, at the Partnership Group, a child-care and elder-care resource and referral service in Lansdale, Pa. "If a dancer can get better by watching herself in the mirror," he notes, "maybe someone who makes a living on the phone can get better by listening to himself."

READER'S CHOICE

Monthly Report Cards

Let's be honest: By the time most of us admit that something's amiss with an employee, it can often be too late to deal with the situation effectively. The nonperformer knows something's wrong, and so do his or her co-workers. And so do you, but you might have ignored the problem until some incident forced you to pay attention.

At Datatec Industries, a Fairfield, N.J., company that installs computer systems in stores, they have **set up an early-alarm system that uses benchmarking to measure each employee's performance.** Datatec measures everything from defects in receivables to late orders to length of service calls. It also requires all employees to rate everyone else's performance either monthly or quarterly. And the final piece of evaluation is provided by the customers, who are surveyed regularly by Datatec for their opinions on service and quality. The results of all this data-gathering are then published monthly for all eyes in the company to see.

As Datatec CEO Chris Carey points out, a new employee knows by the end of the first month how he's doing. The employee sees immediately how he ranks on every aspect of his job, knowing where he needs to improve. Because the surveys are so frequent, any problems are caught early and better performance shows up immediately. And because managers are using the same survey results as workers to evaluate performance, differences in perception are minimized. The strength of Datatec's system is that it allows employees to correct themselves.

The Interactive Employee Review

As a manager for several companies John Strazzanti had lamented the lack of adequate salary review systems. As president of Com-Corp Industries, a Cleveland metal stamper, he wanted to change all that. Strazzanti **wanted his new salary review system to do two things: establish a fair and open standard of pay, and make people feel important and involved.**

So he asked for volunteers for a salary committee and gave the group the job of setting wages by surveying the marketplace to find out what other manufacturers were paying. He also asked all his employees what criteria they thought they should be evaluated on, and incorporated their responses into a scoring system.

Now, three times a year, each Com-Corp employee's technical proficiency and professional attitude are evaluated both quantitatively and qualitatively. All workers are measured not only against their past performance and the goals that have been set for them, but against industry conditions and standards—how the marketplace values their jobs. To encourage improvement, Com-Corp offers instructional classes—from corporate finance to blueprint reading—for those with problems in a given area or for those who want to move up.

The work of the salary committee provides a basis not only to ensure that all employees are paid fairly, but also to track industry trends on job descriptions and the effects of technology on changing job requirements. The whole point of the system is to say, Here's what you can do to make more.

But the review process doesn't end there. Each employee also submits a detailed review of the company's performance three times a year. According to Strazzanti, doing a two-way review three times a year with each employee creates an ongoing dialogue about every aspect of the organization. "Every review, we get suggestions for improvements because people know it will benefit *them* as well as the company."

"The act of firing an employee is one of the crucibles that turn entrepreneurs into managers, because it brings you face-to-face with failure."

Musical Chairs

Looking for a decent way to lay off workers? **Consider the "rotating layoff," which converts such firings from an all-or-nothing proposition into a pain-sharing experience.** Instead of handing out pink slips to a few employees while the rest stay on full-time, all workers participate in a rotating layoff.

Here's how John Leehman, co-owner of Bread Loaf Construction Co., in Middlebury, Vt., designed his accommodative plan: instead of eliminating 10 people from a team of 30, Leehman asks the entire team to work 33% fewer hours by reporting for duty only two weeks out of every three. Leehman "rotates" the layoff week among workers so that Bread Loaf always has 20 team members on hand. "No one loses a job or benefits, and we have a temporary cut in overhead," explains Leehman.

This novel approach has allowed Bread Loaf to attract and keep desirable employees in the notoriously cyclical construction industry, but it could be a solution to unpredictable work flow in other industries, too. Leehman finds that the slight drop in efficiency that results from job switching "is offset by an increase in energy."

Sales Suggestions Anyone?

Boosting sales is everybody's job, even for those who aren't salespeople, at Telecom Library, a 60-employee publishing company, headquartered in New York City. This past winter cofounder Gerry Friesen issued a memo that was a shocker: **layoffs were inevitable, unless everyone pitched in with ideas—not for cost cutting but for gaining more sales.**

It wasn't only the threat of layoffs that got people's attention, but also "the opportunity for them to work directly with me and show their stuff," says Friesen. He listened and asked questions. Then he told employees to flesh out their ideas or explained why they weren't feasible. For promising suggestions, he would always ask, "Do you have time to do this?" If employees said yes, they got the go-ahead.

Editorial employees repackaged a dated but popular book to rejuvenate its sales. Sales staffers exchanged their 50 most-difficult-to-close accounts among themselves. The company got more mileage out of its editorial mailing list by using it to pull together a conference. Six months later, though ad sales are still off, there have been no layoffs, revenues are up, and the company is profitable.

No, Really . . .
You're Fired . . .

Having to work with an unhappy person is hard on everyone, management and co-workers alike. **But can you fire someone simply because of a bad attitude?**

Well, not surprisingly, the answer is yes and no. No state or federal law restricts you from dismissing someone for having a bad attitude if you employ him at-will—that is, if you signed no contract with him or a representative union. But discrimination laws require that you apply performance standards across the board. So if you fired only workers with bad attitudes who are over 40, you're in trouble.

Courts in many states prohibit firing an employee for a reason that counters public policy, such as using a bad attitude as a pretext to fire someone if the real reason is that he filed a workers' compensation claim. Or if it's really because he was a whistle-blower or refused to break the law—to drive an uninspected truck, for example.

Nor can you fire an at-will employee if you guaranteed him job security in an implied contract. Courts may read an implied contract into such verbal statements by managers as, "As long as you get the work done, you'll always have a job here." Even longstanding practices may count: If, in the company's 30-year history, for instance, you've never fired anyone unless he took a torch to the office, you've set a precedent, and you may court trouble by suddenly getting tough and discharging people for "negativity."

But the biggest risk to employers is an employee handbook that lists reasons for termination. Most states will consider that handbook an implied contract that requires adherence. If you fire someone for an unlisted reason, that employee could sue for wrongful discharge. But a good handbook and strict adherence to it can help establish a record that may protect you in court. Sally Tassani, president of Tassani Communications, a Chicago advertising agency, believes "you must document your policy in a handbook and make sure that policy is legal." That's an ongoing process, she cautions. "You can't keep everyone happy, but you do the best you can. State your position clearly, make sure it's legally acceptable, and follow through."

Paying For Results

Firing an employee is bad enough, but it's the economic effect it has on the family that gets Chet Giermak down. For this reason, he changed the discipline policy at his company, Eriez Magnetics, a $55-million industrial-equipment manufacturer in Erie, Pa.

Just as other companies do, Eriez gives employees verbal warnings followed by written ones. If problems persist, many companies then go to the next step—a few days off *without* pay for the employee to think things over.

To Giermak, this last step is not only unnecessarily negative, but doesn't achieve the desired results and penalizes the family unfairly. Instead, Giermak, **after having a personal talk with the employee, tells him to take three days off *with* pay to decide whether he wants to continue to work at the company.**

Giermak believes paying the employee during this probationary period sends just the right signal to the offender and his co-workers. Docking a person's pay can often lead to martyrdom, but paying for days off results in co-workers questioning the offender on how he can play for three days while they work. In the 12 years since the policy was instituted, only 5 people in a workforce that now totals 450 have reached this last step. All 5 asked that the three-days pay be taken out of their paychecks. The money remained in their paychecks, all 5 employees stayed with the company, improved their performance, and no discharges were required.

A Fond Farewell

Most companies prefer to let bygones be bygones when they fire an employee. Ed Steffan, co-owner of EPS Rehabilitation, a rehabilitation and placement service for injured workers in Tinley Park, Ill. has a radically different point of view. "I've always looked at employees as people who are helping me, not expendable objects," he explains. **When things don't work out, he goes to great lengths to help the employee find a new job.**

With only 22 employees, Steffan usually knows if a new hire is going to make it within the first 90 days. If several training attempts to correct deficiencies fail, he tells the worker that the job isn't appropriate and tries to help the employee figure out what's next. A secretary who can't master the medical terminology and personal contact required at EPS, for example, could do very well in a job that requires mostly transcription.

With the employee's job goal set, Steffan often gets the worker's resume updated and printed in-house and alerts his staff to the employee's new job objective. Because EPS has ongoing relationships with its large corporate customers, it can informally poll those organizations for job openings quickly.

Though some employees leave the company with negative feelings, Steffan estimates that he's given concrete help to at least 80% of the 5-6 employees who leave each year. "I see real value in this," he asserts. If a former employee goes to a competitor, Steffan figures he stands to benefit by having that person use EPS as the standard to which he holds his new employer. If the employee goes elsewhere, he'll always be a walking advertisement for the company. Finally, Steffan's ad hoc outplacement effort scores points with the company's customers because it conveys the caring philosophy that EPS uses in serving injured workers.

Avoiding Employee Lawsuits

A layoff may help cut costs in an economic downturn, but these days it's more likely than ever to result in an employee lawsuit. **Business owners can do much to avert such lawsuits by adopting fair employee policies and by documenting their compliance.** Here are some tips and strategies:

• Establish guidelines. All of your company's practices—hiring, promoting, firing—should be codified. You don't need an employee handbook, but it's best to write everything down and make sure everyone gets the message. Explain the criteria and frequency of employee evaluations, and how your company will "discipline" poor job performance. Most important: be frank in performance evaluations.

• Document business conditions. If you see a downturn—and potential layoffs—ahead, you'll have your hands full just keeping your business going. But it will pay to pull together a file that shows relevant events:

The decline. Include objective material such as your financial and bank statements, and letters from major customers who are reducing or stopping their orders. In a brief summary, describe conditions affecting your company and which parts of your company have more employees than are really needed.

The intermediate plan. Before making layoffs, write a plan of action that addresses the slowdown, This might include reducing hours, freezing salaries, and eliminating new hires.

Layoff blueprint. Decide how you'll implement layoffs, including which jobs and in which order. You're safest using the most objective criteria: job skills, performance, attendance, and length of service. Apply your criteria consistently.

The outcome record. Record steps taken in a brief diary entry. Collect records that show your goals were reached.

• Ease the pain. Try to help laid-off employees. You might offer outplacement counseling, give severance pay, or let former employees use your offices to conduct job searches.

All in all, lawsuit protection amounts to being fair—which is what you want to do anyway. But you must be able to demonstrate your equitability to the courts.

"Wrongful-termination
suits filed over the last 20 years
have skyrocketed by more than
2,000% (compared with the
125% that overall civil cases have
grown by in the same period)."

INC. MAGAZINE

Department of Labor Calling

The IRS isn't the only uninvited guest that could show up on your company's doorstep. The Department of Labor (DOL) does investigations, too, looking for minimum wage, overtime, immigration, and child-labor violations.

One of the easiest places to err is in **how you classify employees regarding their eligibility for overtime pay.** Many companies assume that if they pay employees a salary, they don't have to pay overtime. Not so.

The key is knowing who is exempt from overtime pay. The federal and most state governments set a limit of 40 hours a week. Some states require overtime pay after 8 hours a day. While most of the exemption tests are clear enough, others are less so. Below are the three classifications of exempt employees that are fuzziest. Employees in each of these categories must make more than $250 a week. Those making less—but more than $155 a week—must qualify for the more exacting "long form" exemption.

• Professionals. Their primary duty is the performance of work that requires advanced knowledge, including the consistent exercise of discretion. An accountant, for example, uses judgment in deciding whether to expense or capitalize a cost, whereas a bookkeeper may merely adhere to established practices.

• Administrative employees. Their primary duty is office or nonmanual work directly related to management policies or general business operations, and it must include the regular exercise of judgment. Take the tricky case of executive secretaries. Some exercise discretion in ordering furniture, setting up conferences, or choosing vendors, and are thereby exempt. But other executive secretaries are trusted confidantes who type and are privy to highly confidential information. They would not be exempt because they do not use judgment in their jobs.

• Executives. Their primary duty is the management of an enterprise requiring the regular exercise of discretion and supervision of the work of two or more.

If you have misclassified an employee, DOL may ask you to start paying overtime to the employee and ante up with the back pay that you owe. Though less than 10% of violations go to litigation, the DOL wins almost all that do.

A Noncompete with Teeth

The trouble with most noncompete agreements is that they haven't a prayer of holding up in court. They're usually too vague and too restrictive, aiming to provide far more protection than most companies actually need—and far more than most judges will permit. So says Harvey Mackay, chairman and CEO of Mackay Envelope Corp., in Minneapolis.

Mackay's standard agreement has been a success for 25 years—solid in the courtroom and, more important, both effective and fair outside it. Former employees may go to work for another envelope company immediately—with only two restrictions, both of which hold for two years.

Mackay restricts former employees from selling envelopes in only a small area, such as the cities where most of their old accounts were.

Then there's what may be the contract's strongest component: the client list, rendered off-limits after a salesperson leaves Mackay Envelope. "These are valuable accounts," Mackay says. "We want to make it clear that they're Mackay Envelope's property."

The Cost of Sexual Harassment

In the best of possible worlds, sexual-harassment issues would be ironed out the way they have been at Paul Stevens' pasta company Trios—without an harassment policy. When one of his employees was repeatedly pestered by a co-worker, she went to her manager. They then both went to Stevens, who asked them what he should do. They all decided it would be best if the woman confronted the date-seeker herself since she would have to continue to work with him. She did and was never bothered again. End of story.

Stevens was lucky. But his self-correcting atmosphere may not be enough protection for most companies. Under the Civil Rights Act of 1991, a company with fewer than 100 workers can be required to pay up to $50,000 in damages, or higher in some states. The **best advice for small companies is to follow the nearly universally agreed-upon steps to discourage harassment.** It shouldn't be purely a defensive measure. Well-executed policies can help create an ethos of respect in the company—a worthier goal than merely staying out of court. Consider these steps:

• Adopt a sexual harassment policy. Make a personal statement followed by a written document which includes definitions of harassment (consult the EEOC), who must conform, how to report incidents, how grievances will be investigated, and what disciplinary measures will be taken.

• Provide employees with meaningful recourse. Find two neutral yet powerful people to whom employees can bring grievances. Natural choices are the person in charge of the company and another manager or outside advisor. Or give employees the option of complaining to the local office of the EEOC.

• Investigate promptly and take appropriate action. Swift investigation sends strong positive signals to employees, but also can be the best line of legal defense. Once investigated, live up to the promise of stated disciplinary actions.

Strictly Confidential

Safeguarding your company's innermost secrets seems a simple matter of getting employees to sign a nondisclosure agreement. But it's easy to make a misstep. And because the courts in many states are inclined to protect people's rights to pursue their own business opportunities, they may bend over backward to nullify trade-secret provisions, says Eric J. Wallach, a litigation partner at Rosenman & Colin, in New York City.

Trade-secret suits, both actual and threatened, are pervasive in technologically sensitive industries, such as software, as well as nontechnological industries, such as retail discounters. Here's **how to make a trade-secret provision airtight:**

1. Define as narrowly as possible what you want to protect. Whether it's proprietary customers, manufacturing processes, software, or sales formulas, make sure the information cannot be obtained through publicly available sources. If your agreement lumps together the truly proprietary with the merely ordinary, a court may view it as excessively limiting to a former employee and dismiss the whole agreement.

2. Limit the number of people who sign it. While it may seem the safest route is to have all employees pledge their secrecy, it actually makes a trade agreement less enforceable. Ask for signatures from the people you're really concerned about. "If you do it in boilerplate fashion, the court may say you, the employer, clearly haven't thought through where the sensitivity is," says Wallach.

3. Employees should enter into the agreement upon employment. The key ingredient here is that the employee must get something out of a pact. If an employer tries to impose a trade-secret provision after an employee is on board, and gives the employee nothing in return, Wallach says, the courts will strike down the provision. But asking an employee to sign an agreement when she's promoted or given a raise might work.

Protecting Independent Contractor Status

It's well known that the minimalist company's favorite worker—the independent contractor—is under assault by the IRS. **Describing a worker as an independent contractor saves a bundle in pension, group health, and workers' comp expenses, as well as social-security and unemployment taxes. But given the penalties, it pays to know the rules.**

The most common mistake employers make? No written agreements. Contracts should include a statement that the contractor is not eligible for benefits; is free to work elsewhere at any time; and contain a joint severability clause stating that if part of the contract is struck down, the rest of it survives. Also just because someone works at home does not make that person an independent contractor.

Here is a handful of the 19 criteria the IRS uses to classify a worker. A yes answer suggests the worker has the characteristic of an employee, but it's up to an auditor to decide if a number of yes answers calls for a worker reclassification.

• Methodology. Is the worker required to follow the employer's direction about when, where, and how he is to work in order to get the job done?

• Continuing relationship. Does the employer rely on the worker exclusively to perform work at frequently recurring intervals, even when such work is part-time?

• Dispensability. Does the success of the business depend upon the performance/service of the independent contractor?

• Oral or written reports. Is the worker required to submit reports to "account for his actions?"

• Significant investment. Does employer furnish equipment, office space, furniture, machinery, and so forth required by the worker to perform her work?

Not all 19 tests are equally weighted. The most important indicator of "independent" status is whether a worker's services are available to the general public.

If you've misclassified workers, the penalty can range from the amount that should have been withheld to double that. Criminal penalties are far stiffer, a $100,000 fine for a corporation or a year in prison, or both, but are rarely levied. The IRS will often waive penalties if you agree to reclassify workers in the future.

> THE "FATHER OF THE MINIMILL" MANAGES
> NUCOR ACCORDING TO ONE PRINCIPLE:
> SIMPLICITY—SIMPLICITY IN ORGANIZATION,
> COMPENSATION AND STRATEGY

KEN IVERSON

Editor-in-Chief George Gendron conducted this interview with the CEO of Nucor at the company's headquarters in Charlotte, N.C. in late 1985 and it appeared in _Inc._'s April 1986 issue.

Nucor Corp. could very well be the biggest small company in America. Nucor has almost 4,000 employees working in 18 plants around the country, with sales last year of $758 million. For years it has been listed on the _Fortune_ 500. Yet here is a company run by a corporate staff of only 16, working out of 8,000 square feet in an anonymous office building located across the street from a shopping mall on the outskirts of Charlotte, N.C.

There's a modesty and simplicity about this company that reflects its chairman and chief executive officer, F. Kenneth Iverson. Iverson has put the lie to the notion that the American steel industry is dead, with a company that has continued to grow at a compound annual rate of 23% over the past 10 years, selling nothing but steel and steel products. Much of his success derives from a commitment to hands-on management, investment in steel technology, and an unusual compensation program that keeps productivity high, turnover low, and has job applicants lined up around the block.

INC.: In the steel industry, you're something of a renegade for opposing the industry's call for protectionism. Your argument is that protectionism tends to make the industry weaker, not stronger.

IVERSON: That's right. Unless you're under intense competitive pressure and it becomes a question of the survival of the business to do it, you're just going to lapse back into your old ways. There's no other answer. But out of all this will come a lot of things that are beneficial: more of an orientation toward technology, greater productivity, certainly a lot of changes in management structure.

INC.: But isn't the big problem with the American steel industry a wage structure that makes it impossible to compete internationally, no matter how much technology you bring in?

IVERSON: At Nucor we produce more than twice the steel per man-hour as workers in large steel companies. Since we're not unionized, I've heard people say that Nucor is proof that unions per se have a negative impact on worker productivity. That's nonsense! That conveniently ignores vital questions like: What's the quality of direction being given the workers? Where are the resources the workers need to get the job done efficiently? Where's the opportunity for workers to contribute ideas about how to do the job better? The real impediment to producing a higher-quality product more efficiently isn't the workers, union or nonunion; it's management.

INC.: But that's easy for you to say—you don't have to deal with unionized workers with inflexible union wages and work rules. Isn't that the big advantage you have over the integrated mills?

◄ Why Nucor has no unions

IVERSON: Look, I'd be the last to say that unions don't present some problems. But you've got to look at why we don't have unions here. For one thing, we pay our people well. The average hourly worker at our plant in Darlington, N.C., for example, with bonus and everything, earned more than $30,000 last year. In addition, employees know that we are not going to lay anybody off, and that has a tremendous impact on the way people approach their jobs. Many of the work rules that have grown up in the unionized plants—the ones that have led to featherbedding and the resistance to new technology—these are the response to worker demands for some form of job security. Can anyone blame workers for wanting that? I can't. So if there is any responsibility for how these work rules have developed, how they have been negotiated and implemented, I think it belongs with management. At Nucor, we think we've been able to avoid those problems by dealing with the job-security problem right up front.

INC.: The unions aren't at your door, then?
IVERSON: As a matter of fact, the last time we had a union organizer in Darlington, we had to send out management in order to protect the union guy passing out the pamphlets.

We're fortunate—people like to work here. Last fall, Darlington needed eight people, and we put a little ad in the county weekly newspaper that said, "Nucor Steel will take some applications on Saturday morning at 8:30 for new employees." When we went out there for the interviewing, there were 1,200 people lined up in that plant.

INC.: But doesn't that prove the point—that American steelworkers earning $30,000 a year have priced the industry out of business?
IVERSON: And they earn every bit of it. That's one thing I really object to, the people in the large steel companies saying the steelworker earns too much. Sure, it's generous—I would guess it's about 70% more than the average manufacturing worker. But what people forget is that in every industrialized country in the world, the steelworker earns more than the average industrial worker; in Japan, the premium is close to 50%. And there's a reason for it. It's hard, hot, dirty, dangerous, skilled work. We have melters who earn more than $40,000, and I'm just glad they can earn it. But it's not what a person earns in any absolute sense; it's what he earns in relation to what he produces that matters.

INC.: You've said elsewhere that you have absolutely no aversion to hiring a worker who has worked for an integrated steel company. In fact, you like it.
IVERSON: Yeah, we've hired a lot.

INC.: But you won't touch management?

IVERSON: No, because we've not had any success with older management. Now we can hire a fellow who is 40 or under and that will work out OK, because over a period of time we can change him. But older than that we've found that we will never be able to change him.

INC.: In what ways?

IVERSON: Being open to change, for one. Anyone who has worked a certain way, in plants with very rigid rules that have done things the same way for years, has very deeply ingrained habits. It's very hard to break loose from that. We've also found that someone like this has trouble developing the type of communications skills we require between department heads and employees.

INC.: What does that mean?

IVERSON: Well, he has to be willing to get down and communicate with the employees and get them working as a team. He has to do it directly. He can't do it through 14 guys that he builds up between him and the individual, which is how he is used to operating at the big companies.

INC.: That seems to define a significant problem with the steel industry.

Reducing management layers

IVERSON: Yes, and not just in steel. The most important thing American industry needs to do is to reduce the number of management layers. It is probably the single most important factor in a business—the number of layers you have between the foreman and the president of the corporation, for example—because it not only allows you to make decisions faster, it also allows you better communication. That's one thing we are really fanatical about. We have four management layers. We have a foreman, and the foreman goes directly to a department head, and the department head goes directly to the general manager—and he goes directly to this office.

INC.: What's interesting, though, is that if you talk to almost anybody, whether it's an INC.-size company or U.S. Steel, I don't think anyone would

disagree with you. **These things seem to almost develop a life of their own. Organizations seem to breed complexity.**

IVERSON: Absolutely. But it's management's responsibility to fight that tendency. I think there's reason to believe the message is beginning to be heard.

But there's more to it than that. One other important characteristic about Nucor is we try very consciously to eliminate any differentiation between management and everybody else. That's the reason we don't have any assigned parking places, no executive dining rooms. Everybody wears the same colored hard hat. Green is the color you wear. No gold hats for the president.

That hat idea came from me. And after we announced it, I got about four letters from foremen who said something like, "It's my recognition. I put it in the back of my car so everyone can see it! All of my neighbors know I'm a foreman." And I wrote back and was sympathetic but said that the recognition has to come from your leadership ability and not from the color hard hat you wear.

INC.: Along these lines of "recognition," several years ago you were the *Fortune* 500 CEO with the lowest compensation.

IVERSON: Something I was really a little proud of.

INC.: Is that something you communicated to all your employees?

"Share the Pain" program during hard times

IVERSON: You bet your life. That's why, when I walked through a plant during that period of time when we had to cut back to a four-day workweek, or even three and a half days, I never got an employee who complained. His pay may be cut 25%, but he knows the department head is cut more and that the officers are cut, percentagewise, even more. I call it our "Share the Pain" program.

INC.: How do the percentages work out?

IVERSON: Well, it's really a function of our bonus system. If we go to a three-and-a-half-day week, which we have on occasion in order to avoid layoffs, the department head will get cut by 35% to 40%. His bonus is tied to the earnings of that particular plant, which suffer because we're not using equipment efficiently.

And then the officers, at the next level, their salaries are tied in with return on stockholders' equity, and that gets hurt even more when production is cut back. Their total compensation will drop 60% or 70%.

INC.: As was the case for you.
IVERSON: Yes. And that's how it should be. I don't care what the reasons are, but if a company's not successful in one year, excuses don't matter. Management should take the biggest drop in pay because they have the most responsibility.

INC.: Does that make it difficult to recruit good managers?
IVERSON: I'd put it another way. It helps narrow the field to the type of managers we want—someone who has enough confidence in his own abilities that he's sure he's going to make that division succeed.

INC.: Have you ever identified somebody you wanted to hire for whom the compensation policies were an obstacle?
IVERSON: No.

INC.: I can imagine an instance where you have a really good manager doing a good job but, for some reason out of his control, the numbers from a division just are not that good for a given period. Do you ever make up for that with some form of discretionary bonus?
IVERSON: We don't have any discretionary bonuses—zero. It's all based on performance. I really don't want anyone to sit in judgment, because it never is fair. If you're giving a discretionary bonus and it's at the end of the year, you're bound to be influenced by the performance of that individual in the last two or three months. Now maybe something happened to him. Maybe he did great during the first four or five months of the year and then he ran into some family problems at the end. There is no way you can sort that out and be really fair to everyone.

> **Don't have discretionary bonuses, only bonuses based on performance**

INC.: So all your compensation is a function of company performance on

one level or another?

IVERSON: Right. Now in the case of the lowest level, it's the production-incentive compensation that is probably the most important of all. Everything is arranged in groups of 25 to 35 people
who are doing some complete task. For example, in the steel mills,
there are nine bonus groups: there are three in melting and casting,
three in rolling, three in finishing and shipping. Take melting and

> ◀ **Weekly
> production-
> incentive
> compensation**

coating, for example. We start with a base of 12 tons of good billets per hour:
above that, the people in the group get a 4% bonus for every ton per hour. So if
they have a week in which they run, say, 32 tons per hour—and that would be
low—that's an 80% bonus. Take the regular pay, the overtime pay, everything, multiply it by an additional 80%—and we give them that check along with their regular
check the next week.

INC.: So the incentive is right there.

IVERSON: Right. If you work real hard and you get real good performance, you
get the payment for that the next week so that you can very easily relate to the fact
that you worked like a dog and there's the money—not at the end of the year, but
now.

INC.: Is that a system everyone is comfortable with?

IVERSON: It's geared toward performance-oriented employees. There are lots of
people who don't like to work that hard, and they don't last very long with us,
because the rest of the people are not going to let them.

INC.: So the system's really self-policing in a way.

IVERSON: Yeah, it sure is.

**INC.: How does that work out, say, when you start up a new plant with all
new workers?**

IVERSON: It's not unusual for us to have a 200% to 300% turnover the first year.
But once we settle down, and once we've found those performance-oriented individuals, then the turnover rate is almost nothing. The last time we kept track of that, in

a plant with 500 workers, we had 3 people leave in the course of a year. So that's pretty good.

INC.: In addition to performance bonuses, you also have profit sharing. Is there anything unusual about your approach to that?

IVERSON: Well, to a lot of employees, profit sharing was just an abstract idea—it wasn't real money they'd get their hands on one day. Others really believed that the contributions were still the company's money—that we could take it from them at any time and do with it whatever we wanted.

INC.: So what did you do?

IVERSON: Well, we decided we would make part of the profit sharing in cash. It's a small percentage, but along with the regular profit sharing that goes into the trust, we send a check. Well, the

> ◀ **Profit sharing partly paid out in cash**

first time we did it, we made all the checks green because everything in the profit sharing is green—the certificates, the letters, and so on. And we had a bunch of checks that weren't cashed. So I called up the general manager and said, "Charlie, why haven't these 50 checks been cashed?" And so he went out and found that when they got the check, they didn't think it was real, they thought it was something about the annuity they would get at retirement. Some of them threw the checks away, others gave them to the kids to play with. So we replaced them. Now, though, they don't lose them anymore!

INC.: I hear very distinct themes in what you say. At one moment, you talk about the nice touch of paying out a bit of profit sharing in cash, and about your policy of not laying off workers during a recession or a downturn. Another moment, you speak rather matter-of-factly about a compensation system that is almost ruthless when it comes to the question of performance demands.

IVERSON: Don't get the idea that we're paternalistic, because we're really not. This bonus system, for example, is very tough. If you're late even 5 minutes, you lose your bonus for the day. If you're late more than 30 minutes, or you're absent because of sickness or anything else, you lose your bonus for the week. Now, we do have what we call four "forgiveness" days during the year when you can be sick or you have to close on a house or your wife is having a baby. But only four. We have a melter, Phil Johnson, down in Darlington, and one of the workers came in one day and said that Phil had been in an automobile accident and was sitting beside his car off of Route 52, holding his head. So the foreman asked, "Why didn't you stop and help him?" And the guy said, "And lose my bonus?"

INC.: We started this discussion about compensation with your salary, so let's return to that for a moment. Compared with other *Fortune* 500 companies, your executive compensation looks modest.

IVERSON: If we have a good year and we max out, the compensation is really very good. We have no retirement programs, no annuities or anything else; we just have one single plan for officers.

INC.: Profit sharing?

IVERSON: No, officers aren't part of the profit sharing. We have just a single program, a very simple one that's based on stockholders' equity. It kicks in once we reach about 9% return on equity, which is a little below average for manufacturing companies. After **Executive salaries based on ROE** that, 5% of everything that's left over from net earnings [before taxes] goes into a pool for the officers that is then divided up based on their salaries.

INC.: So how does that work out?

IVERSON: Executive salaries are 75% of what they would earn in this industry in comparable positions. Now if return on equity for the company reaches, say 20%, which it has, then we can wind up with as much as 190% of our base in salary and 115% on top of that in stock. We get both.

Of course, that's the maximum. Now in 1982, when we had only a 9% return on equity, it was zero. My base pay right now is $150,000. If we had 20% return on stockholders' equity, all told I'd get about $600,000.

INC.: Not too shabby.

IVERSON: Yeah, but the important thing is if we get only an average return on equity, then the officers are going to earn less than they would in a comparable position.

INC.: Is there a bias in this toward short-term thinking?
IVERSON: You'd think so, but it hasn't worked out that way. You look at all the expansion we've had—the new fastener plant and new deck plant—and the officers get hurt financially in the short term by those. But we're all committed to this company in the long term, so we're willing to make sacrifices today knowing we'll benefit down the road.

INC.: We've talked a good deal about the compensation system. Do you think there may be some limitations on how widely applicable it is to other firms, in other industries?
IVERSON: Limitations? No question about it. To design a system like ours, you have to have two things. First, you have to be able to break out a small group of people who all work as a team on some particular function—by small, I mean maybe 30 to 35 people tops. And in order to give them an incentive, you have to be able to define some measurable product. In our case, it's good billet tons per hour.

INC.: Let's shift gears a little bit. Right now, you're sitting on some $180 million in cash at Nucor, which has caused some speculation on Wall Street that you'll pick up on the trend and go private.
IVERSON: It has been mentioned to us by a number of brokerage firms and investment houses, but we wouldn't even consider it. It wouldn't be fair to the employees, and I don't know whether it would even be fair to the stockholders.

INC.: Why not?
IVERSON: If you go private, then you're going to restrict the growth opportunities of the business because of the burden of carrying so much debt. And in business, you either grow or you die. Oh sure, the officers might make out better under those circumstances, as they usually do in such deals. But certainly the overall company would not be healthier and the opportunities wouldn't be created for people within the company.

INC.: Can we expect you to get into lines other than steel, like others in the industry?

IVERSON: No, we're going to stay in steel and steel products. The way we look at it, this company does only two things well, and that is it builds plants economically and it runs them efficiently. That's the whole company. We don't have any financial expertise, we're not entrepreneurs, we're not into acquisitions. Steel may not be the best business in the world, but it's what we know how to do and we do it well. We're very conscious of that.

EPILOGUE

Very few policies or compensation systems have changed at Nucor since Iverson spoke with *Inc.* back in 1986. Production-incentive compensation is still paid weekly. There are still only four layers of management, and there is now a corporate staff of only 22 for a company of 5,600 employees. Management bonuses remain the same, based on ROE performance. Profit-sharing is still partly paid out in cash. And, still no unions or layoffs despite challenging times in the economy.

What has changed are productivity gains—980 tons per employee in 1986 to 1,300 tons per employee in 1992. (The overall industry average hovers in the 440-ton range.) Also, of the top eight steel producers in the U.S. today, Nucor is the only one that has operated without a loss quarter since 1965.

According to Iverson, one of the biggest challenges facing his business, besides government regulations, is finding good, skilled employees. Since 1986, education has played an ever-increasing role at Nucor, with a newly created position of manager of training and $1 million spent annually on training and basic education. The emphasis on education now goes well beyond the plants. Nucor set up a scholarship program for the children of all employees, paying parents $1,800 a year to help with college costs.

Another emphasis for Nucor today is safety, after unfortunate accidents occurred in the past couple of years, leading Iverson to appoint highly active safety coordinators in each of the 23 plants.

JACK STACK

Executive Editor Bo Burlingham met with the CEO of Springfield Remanufacturing Corp. at the company headquarters in Missouri in mid-1989, working up this report for the October 1989 issue of *Inc.*

Here's the plot: A middle manager at one of America's worst-run companies is sent on a mission to shut down an ailing plant in Springfield, Mo. The guy is barely 30 years old, a college dropout. When he shows up at the plant, he finds a work force so demoralized the only real question is whether the Teamsters or the United Auto Workers will win the upcoming union election. Somehow he is able to rally the workers, stave off the union, and save the plant. Four years later he buys the division with his fellow managers and builds it into the star of its industry, using an original—some would say revolutionary—approach to management.

Such is the unlikely saga of Jack Stack, a man who has fascinated us ever since we met him in 1985, less than three years after he negotiated the leveraged buyout of Springfield Remanufacturing Corp. (SRC) from International Harvester Corp. At the time he was still in the process of inventing what came to be known as the Great Game of Business, SRC's unique management system, but we could already see he was onto something. His way of running a company seemed so simple, so logical, so obvious that it was hard not to wonder, Why isn't every business run this way?

Stack's approach is based on the premise that business is essentially a game—one that is no more complicated than, say, baseball or football, probably less. Yet most people don't understand it, he argues, because they've never been taught the rules. At SRC everyone learns the rules and plays the Game, from the receptionist at the front desk to the guy who cleans engine parts. They follow the action through weekly income statements and react accordingly, homing in on their annual goals. They also share in the risks and rewards: how they perform determines both the size of their quarterly bonuses and the value of their stock.

It's a system that transforms every aspect of the business, from compensation to marketing to finance. Its effectiveness is a tribute to its creator, Jack Stack. Yet as extraordinary as Stack is in one way, he is typical of a whole generation of managers in another. After all, he didn't set out to be the chief executive officer of a $50-million company with 475 employees. In the course of becoming one, he's had to deal with a range of difficult issues.

INC.: I think most company presidents we know get a certain charge out of occupying the top slot, despite all the aggravations. Do you like being the boss?

Reflections on being the boss

STACK: Well, no, not really. Because a boss is forced to set examples, and I'm not a good example setter. I really don't like living in a glass house. People pay a lot of attention to the guy who's in charge. What he says is always being compared with what he does. And that's the way it should be. If I'm going to say something, I'll do it, too. But I'd rather not be under that microscope, because I know one day I'm going to slip.

INC.: Are you worried that the company will turn on you?
STACK: I hope not. I've worked pretty hard to keep that from happening.

INC.: What do you mean?
STACK: Well, you can go back to the buyout. I don't own 100% of SRC. I own 19%. The rest is owned by the employee stock ownership plan and various employees. I could have had more, but that was plenty for me. Not wanting to be accused of being greedy probably had something to do with it. But more important, I didn't

want to be alone. I was going to be leading the charge up the hill. I wanted to make sure that when I got to the top of the hill and turned around, there was a bunch of people coming with me.

INC.: A lot of company founders would say you're crazy. Do you really think you're safer as a minority stockholder than as the sole owner?
STACK: I've learned that there are certain higher laws in business. One of them is "You get what you give." And here's another: "It's easy to stop one guy, but it's pretty hard to stop 100." I don't know where I got these laws. You don't learn them in college. You pick them up on the street. I probably got them from supervising 2,000 or so people at International Harvester and then here. But I know they are real laws.

INC.: It sounds as though you had already developed a lot of your ideas about business before you came to Springfield.
STACK: Absolutely. I learned a lot at Harvester.

INC.: Give us an example.
STACK: One of my first big lessons was in 1972 or '73. I remember, we had to ship out 800 tractors to the Soviet Union, and I was in charge of scheduling the parts. At the time there was a severe shortage of the parts we needed, but without those parts the tractors wouldn't go to Russia, and our department would get killed. As I recall, we had until November 1, and this was October already. On paper, it couldn't be done. So I put up a big sign, saying "OUR GOAL: 800 TRACTORS," and I explained to my guys exactly what was going on, what was at stake. That was unusual, because Harvester was a very quiet company. I'd go to meetings, and the understanding was always, OK, here's what we have to do, but don't tell anybody.

INC.: How did your people respond?
STACK: They were amazing. They went into the factory each night and crawled over those tractors and figured out what parts were needed and how many tractors were short those particular parts. Then they got the parts any way they could. On October 31, we hit 803. Boy, did we send up the balloons.

INC.: Why was that such an important lesson to you?

STACK: Because it showed me what people could do. I saw these guys get hungry. I saw them push and accomplish things they never thought were possible. I saw satisfaction on a daily basis. I mean, these guys didn't know they were working! I thought, My

> The secret to increasing productivity

God, if I can get people pumped up, wanting to come to work every day, what an edge that is! That's what nobody else is doing. Suppose I could run the right numbers, so that a guy wakes up in the morning and says, "Man, I feel like shit, but I really want to go in there and see what happened." That's the whole secret to increasing productivity.

INC.: In a way, that's the definition of a good boss, isn't it? Someone who creates an atmosphere where people want to come to work in the morning.

STACK: I guess. Anyway, it absolutely convinced me that secrecy is bullshit. From then on, I was going to give my people everything I've got, and eventually that grew into the whole idea of teaching people how to make money.

INC.: Wait a minute. You're getting ahead of us here. What do you mean, "teaching people how to make money"?

STACK: Well, think about it. Most people who work in companies don't understand business. They have all kinds of misconceptions. They think profit is a dirty word. They think the owners just slip it into their bank accounts at night. They have no idea that 46% of business profits goes to taxes. They've never heard of retained earnings. And there's a good reason for all this ignorance. No one teaches them how business works. I worked at the Harvester plant in Melrose Park, Ill., for 10 years. Every Friday I went to a staff meeting where the plant manager said, "We gotta make more money, we gotta be more profitable." But he never taught me *how* to make more money. We got plenty of orders—deliver a crankcase to such-and-such line, make sure that workers are safe, get so-and-so's productivity up. I never knew anything about making money, and here I'd supervised hundreds and hundreds of people. Finally, it dawned on me that there was a better way.

INC.: Which is . . .

STACK: It's the way businesses have been run for a long, long time—with financial statements. If people know how to use them, that's really the simplest way to run a business.

INC.: Hold on. Say I'm 23 years old with a high-school education and an entry-level job at SRC. You're going to teach me to read financial statements?

STACK: That's right. When people come to work at SRC, we tell them that 70% of the job is disassembly or whatever and 30% of the job is learning. What they learn is how to make money, how to make a profit. They don't have to play the game, but they do have to learn it. We teach them about aftertax profits, retained earnings, equity, cash flow, everything. We teach them how to read an income statement and a balance sheet. We say, "You make the decision whether you want to work here, but these are the ground rules we play by."

Then every week the supervisors come back with the updated income statement, showing how we're doing in relation to our annual goals. And of course, the quarterly bonuses are tied to those goals. So the numbers are just flying around. The more people understand, the more they want to see the results. They want to know how well they are doing and if they are contributing.

◀ **Introducing The Great Game of Business**

There's internal competition and peer pressure, and they get caught up in it. It's a game—the Great Game of Business, as we call it. It's a mechanism for getting people to come into work every morning and enjoy it.

INC.: Did you start out with this idea of teaching people how to make money?

STACK: No, I started out with the idea that I really didn't want to be in the position of having to lay people off.

INC.: What do you mean?

STACK: I just think you take on a big obligation when you hire somebody. That person is bringing home money, putting food on the table, taking care of children. You can't take that lightly. Of course, it's a two-way street, but—as much as possible—you should make it their choice whether they leave or not.

INC.: OK, but what does that have to do with your Game?
STACK: That's how the Game got started. After the buyout, we had an 89-to-1 debt-to-equity ratio. As a corporate entity, we were nearly comatose. We began with $1 million in working capital, but we owed $8 million, and all the assets were pledged. So I looked at this situation, and I realized there were two things we couldn't do. Number one, we couldn't run out of cash. Number two, we couldn't destroy ourselves from within. If either one of those happened, we'd lose the company, and 165 people would lose their jobs.

INC.: How might the company have destroyed itself from within?
STACK: Bad morale. The danger was we'd get into a situation where people would turn on each other. So how do you avoid that? It became obvious to me that we had to communicate with people through the financial statements. They had to know the company's situation at every point. We had to tell them where the cash was and then make sure they were involved in deciding what to do with that cash. That's how the Game evolved.

INC.: In a sense, you're saying this system provides people with a kind of job security.
STACK: It provides them with the only kind of job security that means anything. Look at Harvester—a company that went back 100 years, one of the 30 largest in the country, more than 100,000 employees. My dad retired from it. I worked there for 14 years altogether. I just assumed my job was secure, and I had no way of knowing it wasn't. Then Harvester went down the tubes. So that's one thing the Game does: it gives people a scorecard and a way to influence the score. It tells them how secure their jobs really are. It doesn't provide guarantees, but there aren't guarantees anymore.

INC.: At the same time, it reduces your responsibility for their job security, doesn't it?
STACK: It delegates the responsibility, yes. Just like it delegates every action in the

company. It doesn't put all the emphasis on one guy.

INC.: How does it delegate every action in the company?
STACK: By identifying each person's role. Our people know exactly where they show up on the income statement and how they contribute. So responsibilities are completely delegated. The Game provides a structure whereby the individuals support the body. It teaches people the fundamentals—what they each have to do to make the company successful. If your fundamentals get out of whack, you find out right away, and you don't move until they're back in line.

> The Game delegates every action in the company

INC.: Who makes sure that you don't move?
STACK: Usually, it's your peers.

INC.: If all these responsibilities are delegated, what does that mean for you as the boss?
STACK: My role is to make sure the Game is working. For example, we have two companywide goals every year. One is profitability, and the other changes from year to year, depending on the particular weakness we see in the company. This year we've targeted liquidity, measured as current assets divided by current liabilities.

INC.: Why liquidity?
STACK: It's something we don't have under control, and it's the only thing that can really hurt us. We have to control the spending. Otherwise, if we grow too quickly, we're going to run out of cash. If we run out of cash, we're not going to have a company—or rather, the company is not going to be ours anymore. We'll have to bring in somebody to put in the cash we need to grow, and that will change the Game. OK, so we completely missed our liquidity target in the first quarter. Now it's true that you often don't hit your targets right away if you've picked a really good goal. The whole idea is to choose a weakness that affects your long-term security. If you solve the problem too easily, it may not be a real weakness. But even so, you expect some progress in the first quarter. In this case, the progress was very disappointing.

INC.: Whose fault was that?

STACK: I think it's my responsibility to make sure those goals are met. I mean, we're talking about a major problem that affects the long-term security of the employees. If the problem isn't being solved, I need to do everything I possibly can to get the organization focused on it. So we put together a high-level task force to reduce inventory—I'm talking about really visible people in important positions around the company. We pulled them off their jobs to focus on this particular problem. At the same time, we straightened up accounting to make certain we're 100% on top of all our receivables. Of course, this sends a message. It creates an atmosphere where everybody is working toward the same goal and doing their part to get the bonus.

INC.: It's interesting that your Game relies so heavily on incentive compensation systems, and yet what really inspires you is getting people to work for rewards other than money.

STACK: I'm not foolish enough to believe that money isn't a major motivator. It just isn't necessarily the only one. I guess what I'm really obsessed with is getting rid of the living dead. I can't stand going into factories and businesses and seeing all these faceless people around. They don't look healthy, and they don't act healthy, and they're a big problem for corporate America.

INC.: Faceless people?

STACK: The people who are there because it's a job, whose attitude is "I have to be here, but I don't have to like it. I'll do it for my family, not for myself." You can't believe how I hate this. What have we done to create those kinds of environments? We should be able to tell this person, "It's your *obligation* to be happy. Find somewhere to be happy. Don't sit around me and be miserable." Then we wonder why we have a productivity problem. Well, you can't have high productivity with faceless people. They're not happy with themselves, they're not happy with their jobs, they bring you down. So what do we do? I mean, there are lots of jobs in this world that involve putting washers on bolts. You can't walk away from it. The work is boring, but it has to be done. I think the answer is a system where everybody can have fun, even the people who put washers on bolts. They can be playing something else at the same time. Statistics, rewards, and incentives are one way to do that—to make people aware, to stimulate them, to give them the opportunity to use their intelligence and achieve something.

INC.: Let me play devil's advocate. We often see incentive systems that have the opposite effect, that become a mechanism of control and that make work less fun, not more.
STACK: That happens if you have shortsighted or unquantifiable goals. You need goals with a larger meaning.

INC.: In what sense?
STACK: Our goals are always based on the security of the company, so the larger meaning is to create jobs and keep people working. If we fail to reach a goal, the company is at risk. Each goal is a must, not a want. I mean, we're trying to create a company that will last 30, 40, 50 years. More important, we're creating a system that makes everybody aware of the company's strengths and weaknesses and that forces the weaknesses to be addressed.

INC.: You say the larger meaning is to create jobs. Why isn't it to create top-quality products for customers?
STACK: There's another higher law, which is "If you are going to take care of other people, you have to take care of yourself first." That applies to the company. If our people don't feel good about themselves, they aren't going to be good at re-manufacturing engines. The more time they spend in training programs, education, getting involved, the better the end product is going to be. They have to be in the right frame of mind, free of mental stress; they can't be worrying about their job security. Happy people are productive people, and productive people do all the little things required to be great at remanufacturing. That's what the Game is all about.

INC.: But can't you focus too much on making people feel good about themselves? We know of companies that got so involved with corporate culture and self-improvement they forgot about their customers.
STACK: There's a big difference between what we do and what you're talking about.

Those companies get caught up in a kind of emotionalism. We do the opposite. Our Game takes emotions out of the business. We go by the statistics, and the statistics don't lie. Emotions can get you all screwed up. We train our people to see that success means making sure one plus one comes out to two. It has nothing to do with standing in a circle and doing a real good job of falling into someone else's arms. We're talking about income statements and balance sheets, not about cafeterias and parking spaces.

INC.: I noticed the top managers at SRC have reserved parking spaces.
STACK: Well, partly, that's a carryover from Harvester, but it is a luxury, no question. I think there have to be certain perks that come with certain jobs, because you want people to want to get ahead. If we treated everyone equally, why would anyone want to take on additional responsibility?

INC.: But you can use that logic to justify enormous disparities of income, equity, fringe benefits, whatever.
STACK: A good manager knows what the guy on the shop floor absolutely can't stand and has disdain for. There is a definite flash point on fringe benefits. Common sense really needs to prevail. If I buy a factory one day and show up in a Lamborghini the next, can I then go and talk about the company being at risk? Would anyone believe me? The point is that you always have to maintain credibility. That requires a sixth sense, one that tells you when your credibility is in question. You know it. You can hear it out on the shop floor. You can feel it. To be a good manager, you have to have that sixth sense.

INC.: You're saying that one of your main jobs is to anticipate credibility problems before they arise.
STACK: Absolutely, especially when you're talking about the bonuses. That's why it was so important for us to take action on the liquidity goal even before the first-quarter results were in. We knew that the first question people were going to ask the frontline supervisors was "What are we going to do to get the bonuses?" We had to prepare an answer for them, and it had to be good one. And the answer was "OK, we blew it, but we're dead serious, and we're committing top people and about

$300,000 in resources toward solving the problem. This is not going to be a part-time attack. This is going to be a full-time attack for the next three quarters."

INC.: Can we go back to your point about taking emotions out of the business? A lot of people would argue that businesses thrive on emotion, that companies don't do enough to motivate employees, that we need more pom-poms and inspiration, not less.

STACK: Don't get me wrong. I'm really big on pom-poms and celebrations and inspirational messages. I just don't think they should replace solid information about the condition of the company. People should understand why those pom-poms are there. It's not fair to pat workers on the back all the time, telling them what a great job they're doing and what a great company this is, and then two years later close the door on them. They deserve more than that. They deserve to evaluate the situation for themselves. I don't want people to sit there and passively accept leadership. I want them to become active in leadership, and that means giving them a constructive path to follow. I don't think management should be some kind of glorified cheerleader.

> **◀ Motivating people by giving them solid information**

INC.: OK, so you go by the numbers. But haven't you ever gotten into a situation where the numbers tell you to do one thing and your heart wants you to do something else?

STACK: Do I ever feel torn? Yes, of course. I felt incredibly torn after General Motors canceled those 5,000 engines in December 1986. I mean, the numbers said we had to cut 100 people from the payroll or risk the company. But that kind of layoff would have been a tremendous failure of management. There was nobody else to blame. You've got to take responsibility, even if there was no way you could have seen it coming.

INC.: I guess that decision wasn't much fun.

STACK: Aw, no, it was awful. Because you're deciding whether to take somebody's job away. You could protect your own ass. But you'd sit there and stare at the ceiling and think about these people who were told they had a job. It should be their choice, not yours.

INC.: What did other people think?

STACK: There was a small group of senior employees who didn't want to take the chance. They weren't close to the new group, the ones who would be laid off. They said, "Hell, if it's between me and them, let it be them." And they had a very good point. In order to get by without a layoff, we would have to get 100 new product lines up and running in three months. Well, you just can't introduce products that fast. And if we failed, we would have had to do a much bigger layoff, get a new infusion of outside capital, and change the whole thinking of the company. It's possible there would have been a change in management as well.

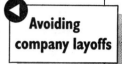

Avoiding company layoffs

INC.: So what happened?

STACK: Eventually those senior people came around. That's probably what sold me more than anything else. The hard-core guys came back and said, "Jeez, we've been thinking about it, and we can weather it. We'll have to train these kids, but we'll make it. We can do it."

INC.: Was that an emotional decision?

STACK: No, I think they'd figured it out statistically. We told them we thought it was an impossible task, but they could break down the elements of the job in more detail than we could. I guess they just realized they had 33% more left.

INC.: You must feel pride in the way you dealt with that situation.

STACK: I don't know. I think the system took care of itself. If I'd heard something else from the organization, I might have had to react differently. But when those guys said, "Let's try it," that was all I needed. I really wanted to go that way. When you can see compassion in your fellow workers, that's a big reward. It motivates you even more, because you see what a good group you're working with.

INC.: What was it like to introduce all those new lines?

STACK: It was pure hell. We told people that the pressures would be overwhelming, but I don't think we had any idea how overwhelming they were really going to be. We cried in July, it was so rough. We couldn't get our quality up. We couldn't get our routines together. We had severe start-up problems. It was like recovering from a stroke—very slow and very painful, and it hurt. It really hurt. I'm talking about long-term pain. I think we're only getting over it now.

INC.: But you made it without any layoffs.
STACK: Yeah. In fact, we added 100 people.

INC.: It's interesting that you feel so strongly about letting employees decide whether to stay or leave, about letting it be their choice. You must have a hell of a time firing people.

Firing unhappy people

STACK: Well, I don't want to work around unhappy people, and if people aren't happy, I don't mind telling them that they're unhappy and they should go somewhere else. Of course, you have to understand, I really don't have to fire many people. This system does a lot of the work. The nonperformers take themselves out. Peer pressure takes them out. But, yes, anytime somebody leaves, you feel the loss.

INC.: Even the deadwood?
STACK: Deadwood is such a small percentage. It's the ones with talent who are really tough. But even losing deadwood is tough because you spend a lot of time and money training, teaching, and motivating them.

INC.: How do you deal with the talented ones?
STACK: That's probably the most stressful part of my job. I mean, when you know a guy has incredible talent but you just can't harness it, you can't focus it, you can't get it into the system—it kills you. And then, of course, you start questioning whether the problem is him or you. You start saying to yourself, "Maybe we just have a style conflict here. Maybe I'm being too possessive. Maybe I don't want to let go." Fortunately, the system serves as a reality check.

INC.: In what way?

STACK: A style conflict won't necessarily show up in the numbers. A performance problem becomes very clear very fast, and everybody knows about it. Then the pressure gets intense. You have to do something. I can't explain to 450 people why we didn't deal with a situation—not if it costs them their bonuses.

INC.: Is there anybody you can talk to about those kinds of issues?
STACK: I think I talk to everybody. We're all very, very close.

INC.: Are you saying that it really isn't so lonely at the top after all? I mean, what's the difference between being the number-one person and being number two, three, or four?
STACK: First, let me say there isn't always a distinct number two, three, and four. In the past decade especially, people have become very coy about designating a chain of command. It gets in the way of building a team. You can say who does what when you're gone, but you can't go much beyond that without undermining team spirit. Now in that context, the number-one person has to be prepared to work exclusively on deviations and problems. If something is going right, you have to let it go right, no matter how good you may be at that aspect of the business. Otherwise, you can't function as number one, because your role as number one is to focus on what's going wrong. When the numbers show there's a problem, you've got to go in and make sure it gets fixed, and that could be anything—quality, volume, sales, inventories, bad debt, extension of receivables, whatever.

INC.: I suppose, if you keep delegating enough responsibilities, you could make yourself obsolete.
STACK: My *job* is to make myself obsolete, and I'm getting there. In many ways, I'm not the boss of SRC anymore. Our system is the boss.

EPILOGUE
One thing that can be said about SRC's Great Game is that there's apparently never a dull inning—or a scoreless one, for that matter. The company today employs more than 650 people with estimated revenues of $82 million

for 1992. The growth of the past decade has taken its toll on people at SRC, who, says Stack, "are simply exhausted. We really need two years to catch our breath." And so the company has come up with a clever solution. On the one hand, SRC has vowed not to expand its product lines; in other words, it has temporarily capped the volume of its existing businesses.

At the same time, however, it has begun to spawn *new* businesses. In order to provide more opportunities for the employees of SRC, there is now an open invitation to all those at the company to suggest start-up possibilities for which SRC will provide the seed capital. In the past couple of years, 12 businesses have been started and are being run by people who received their business education at SRC. As these minnows grow, the 'employee owners' have the option of buying out SRC's share of the equity. These future buyouts will then increase the equity of the employees-stockholders of SRC itself. As Stack explains it, "Now we are getting a new lesson in the power of multiple."

Meanwhile, the company has taken to teaching the Great Game of Business to more than just its own employees. Suppliers, customers, even visiting *Fortune* 500 companies, are all adapting the Game for themselves. One SRC start-up business, Executive Institute, allows anywhere from 10 to 30 executives from other companies to spend several days at SRC observing how the Game works first-hand—kind of a spring training for business leaders.

In order to handle the requests for information about the Game (as well as have a comprehensive description to hand out to new SRC employees), Stack took to working on a book with the former Executive Editor of *Inc.*, Bo Burlingham. Its title, of course, *The Great Game of Business*, published in 1992. All proceeds from the book go back into SRC to buy equipment and finance new businesses.

As to the question of Stack's personal obsolescence that ended the original interview, Stack does admit to a bit of jealousy as he watches SRC colleagues spin themselves off. "You know, what I love is the factory floor," says Stack. "So I've started to fantasize about this little manufacturing company I'm going to buy. I can see it now...It's a disaster, the odds against it making it are overwhelming..."

3

> BY BRINGING HUMANITY BACK INTO BUSINESS,
> THE BODY SHOP HAS BEEN ABLE TO AROUSE
> FEELINGS OF ENTHUSIASM AND COMMITMENT
> AMONG ITS CUSTOMERS AND STAFF
> MORE COMMON TO A POLITICAL MOVEMENT
> THAN A CORPORATION

ANITA RODDICK

Editors George Gendron and Bo Burlingham traveled to England to meet with the founder of The Body Shop International in Dec. 1989. This interview was subsequently worked into a piece which appeared in the June 1990 issue of *Inc.*

Here it is, the start of another bloody *brilliant* decade, and Anita Roddick is worried. So what if *Vogue* anointed her the queen of the beauty industry? So what if her chain of eco-conscious cosmetic stores is the toast of England, counting the likes of Princess Di and Sting among its boosters? So what if her company's shares continue to trade at a frigging 50 times earnings on London's stock exchange? These matters are of no interest to Roddick as she charges through headquarters of The Body Shop International, the company she founded in a storefront 14 years ago.

What worries her is a creeping fat-cat mentality that comes with success. And if success is at the root of Roddick's anxiety, she has cause for concern. For over a decade, sales and profits have continued to grow on average 50% a year. By the end of fiscal 1990, pretax profits had climbed to an estimated $23 million on sales of $141 million. But that's just the beginning. The company has barely begun to tap its potential overseas. It now operates in 37 countries, with a number of foreign operations approaching a critical mass a retail chain needs to explode in a market. And the company is now beginning its big push into the United States, with Japan set to follow.

What's even more extraordinary than The Body Shop's growth record, however, is the effect the company has on the people who come in contact with it. Indeed, it arouses feelings of enthusiasm, commitment, and loyalty among customers and staff more common to a political movement than a corporation. Franchisees, employees, and managers talk about the difficulty they would have going back to work in an "ordinary" company.

The Body Shop is almost as well known for its passionate environmentalism and its trade links with the Third World as for its cosmetics and lotions. It has used its shops worldwide as the base for a series of highly visible campaigns to save the whales, stop the burning of the rain forests, and so on. Such activism has, if anything, enhanced The Body Shop's mystique. Once viewed as an intriguing but irrelevant remnant of the 1960s, it has increasingly come to define the mainstream. Far from a curiosity, The Body Shop has now become a symbol of new business consciousness.

But this activism does not totally explain the attraction of The Body Shop, not even when coupled with a personality as dynamic as that of Anita Roddick or a manager as capable as her husband, Body Shop chairman Gordon Roddick. So where does the electricity come from? Its success raises questions, not just about technique and strategy, but about some of the most fundamental aspects of business.

INC: Anita, the growth of The Body Shop has been staggering by anyone's standards, but you yourself believe so strongly that giantism can be a destructive force for a company?
RODDICK: What frightens me about giantism relates to my very real belief that mediocrity is everywhere. I can see it. You can smell it in the air. And the larger a corporation is, often mediocrity

How giantism can affect the standards of a company

creeps into the thinking. Where I am nervous for me is that giant thinking leads to lack of risk, lack of soul, where nobody is ultimately responsible. We have now got hundreds of stores. We can't make a mistake. Because if we make a mistake, it is mega, mega, mega. It's that type of thinking that could come through.

What we are doing—and I think very well—is constantly breaking down those edges of thinking.

INC: Don't you reach a certain point or certain scale, where you have to standardize to some extent?

RODDICK: Of course, to some extent, but you can standardize for originality. You don't have to standardize for mediocrity. It all starts with recruiting. Using absolute care in choosing the right people, people who fit into the company. You want people who love you and love the values of your company. You don't want confrontation all the time. Also you don't want people who just have a sense of their own growth, not others' or the company's.

We have a pretty extensive process for hiring—a long questionnaire to understand a person's values and interests and, in the case of store managers or franchisees, our management interviews them, as does five full groups within the company—trainers, retailers, franchising, manufacturing, environmental.

INC: Do you think the consequences of this giantism you are concerned with is strictly a function of size?

RODDICK: No, not completely. It's mainly due to lack of communication. That's why The Body Shop revolves around communications and information, both to the staff and to our customers. We just inundate them with printed and visual materials— monthly videos and weekly newsletters about the company and issues of concern. And remember, we are very global. We are constantly moving around. 30% of my job is visiting stores around the

How The Body Shop communicates with its staff and customers

world and talking to staff. That's not only myself. There is a whole group of my staff, based in England, that do the same.

Also, I am a real believer in the printed word. It's not enough to just say, "Let's be special, you guys." I think when you print things up and put them on the walls or plaster them on your distribution trucks, whether it's quotes from Mahatma Gandhi or Joseph Campbell, it reinforces a message that whatever you do in this environment is worth doing. I've just commissioned a whole series of paintings for the warehouse on the enemies of the body. A huge, electric painting explains with pithy statements how many people die from lung cancer or whatever it is. Now you cover a whole warehouse or a whole office with that type of information, you get to know what the values of the company are pretty well.

Another strong way of sending messages out to a wide audience is stuffing them into a person's pay packet. That's the most direct form and it's usually always read. We're trying to do more of that these days too.

INC: You've taken the printed word and graphics to an art form when it comes to communicating. Where does all this stem from?
RODDICK: I've taken what every good teacher knows. And a good teacher I was. You keep your audience; you keep your staff enthralled by human anecdotes. You keep your classroom enthralled by making it the most aesthetically pleasing room. I've haven't done anything different from what I was doing as a teacher. Because when I was a history teacher, everywhere around me there were graphics. I mean brilliant, whether it was just taking the eye and blowing it up of James I and putting it there with a quote. Playing music of the era the whole time. The kids had the right, if they were bored with what I was doing, to just get up and walk around the room and make notes from the presentation.

Now I'm doing nothing different in the warehouse or in the shops. There is education there, environment there, there are anecdotes on the products. And anecdotes adhere, little bits of information. That's how we're learning these days. So, it's really back to what I knew how to do well. It's a show. It's a stage.

INC: Besides the visual messages which convey the company's values and priorities, you also have a pretty extensive formal training program. Let's say someone gets hired as a salesperson in one of the stores, a kid, by a franchisee. What control do you have over her?
RODDICK: Training, everything. I mean everything. We believe

◄ **The Body Shop's training programs**

education is the cornerstone by which we are surviving. There is a training package and an induction package that takes three months and is controlled through our training department.

INC: How does it work logistically? Are they selling while they're doing it?
RODDICK: Oh, yes, it will be like an hour or two a day. Each shop has its own trainer who has come here for formal training courses themselves. The new person learns all about the company, the products, product development, biology of the skin, customer care.

Then there are induction courses here at the headquarters, with thousands passing through each year. We've now got so many to do we've begun to take road shows out into areas where it is difficult for the staff to come to London. But if they do come to London, which will mainly be our England-based store staff, we have over 30 courses for them.

Of course, we also have training videos. We have four or five product training videos—seeds, nuts, oils, herbs, whatever. And I think we've done the most brilliant video called "Smile, Damn It, Smile" on customer care, which is excellent. Every shop has that.

INC: Does the training process stop after the three months?
RODDICK: Oh, no. There's also manager's training—learning management skills through acting courses and also more formal training, 34 courses in all, which have a lot to do with consciousness-raising as well.

The opportunity for training and courses is ongoing for anyone at The Body Shop. One of the reasons we're moving is for larger educational facilities. We're setting up a night school with continuing education classes and literacy classes. We're also bringing in people from around the world to talk to our managers and staff—people who we feel are on the cutting edge of anything we think is interesting.

The night school will also lessen the division of myself. By that I mean, I can't be here as much as some would like. I've got to go source products in the Third World, set up trade initiatives, set up stores, visit stores in Australia, the Arctic Circle, Canada, America. I'll be organizing a lot of the curriculum for the night school, so I'll be present that way.

INC: Lots of people will read this and say, "That's fine, they can do it, but they make millions of pounds a year."
RODDICK: Yes, but we always did training without formalizing it. I always had managers' meetings and staff meetings devoted to training and it gradually just grew into a department of the company. We've always thought of education as an investment not an expense.

INC: Just to back up a second. You just mentioned how your staff is disturbed about the fact that you're not around enough? Obviously another concern you have about giantism?

> The most crucial job of any CEO

RODDICK: Oh, sure. The fact that I'm here, but not often enough, is cause for them to say, "We never see you. You are always going off to other shops around the world or whatever." It's that cry which is the most stressful thing I have to deal with.

In the old days, we had our Christmas parties in my mom's front room. Everybody stayed with us. Well, obviously, all that's changed. That's why all the communications and the education is so important to keep people involved and motivated. And I tell you, motivating is one of the most crucial jobs of any person running a company. Forget about creating and keeping a customer. That's what I used to think my job was. It is motivation. It's motivation and leadership, and it's not a leadership which says, "I'm here and you're all behind me." It's a leadership which says, "You guys. I only got 5-O levels. I'm a kid from an immigrant family."

INC: 5-O levels?
RODDICK: That's a standard before you even get to high school, let's say, or university or something. "Everything is possible. Just everything." That's what I think leadership should be. Not just pushing your own ideas down, but basically saying, "Hey, everything was possible for me and it can be for you too."

INC: What formal incentives does The Body Shop use to help motivate staff?
RODDICK: Well, that's also been a lesson in communications. One night I was out

to dinner with some staff from a store and someone mentioned how they'd been working for the company for four years, but hadn't received much over and above their salary. I said, "What? What about your bloody share options? What about the fact that you're now on six weeks holiday?" Their response, "Share options? Oh, we don't understand it." I said, "What did you do? You've got your one pound to buy your 200 shares." Well, they just use their share-option money to buy lagers instead.

> **Communicating benefits and incentives**

Immediately, I knew we hadn't communicated. I get awards for communication, but what we haven't done well is communicating the business of the business to them. They don't know what a profit and loss statement is. They don't understand what a share is. So now we're addressing a whole new training need.

Beyond the formal motivational initiatives, we're also always trying to research and test out more extraordinary gestures.

INC: Like what?

RODDICK: Well, for example, we've got one franchisee who said to his staff, "You've got an option. You work so wonderfully. You can have your three-weeks bonus or we can send all of you to India for two weeks." The impact this has on these girls, many of whom have never left their town before, is stupendous. The franchisee masterminded the whole thing—got group leaders, hosts in each city—brilliant.

INC: You've said that every great business is a family business. Why is that?

RODDICK: What's so good about family? Well, for one thing, you trust them. We constantly try to create a family atmosphere here and one way that helps is literally hiring whole families. We have sons, mothers, fathers, daughters working for us in small groups all around the company. We try to do the same in the owner-operated franchise stops. Now, if we come back to my original concern about giantism in business, I think we are doing a great job fighting the large company feel by humanizing it with family involvement. You talk about the business at home and it becomes this whole new part of the family.

INC: This whole approach that you have towards your business, is this something that can be replicated everywhere in the economy? You happen to be in a very peculiar niche—personal products, intimacy....

RODDICK: I think it is. That's the big argument large corporations will tell us, "It's okay for you." That's ridiculous. You can humanize any business. Let's take H.J. Heinz. Nobody ever talks about the founding spirit of H.J. Was he a shit, a renegade, brilliant? What did he do to make the company what it is today? Nobody talks about that. If I owned a large corporation, I'd do everything I had to to humanize it, from the history, the rituals, the language, the creation of myth, the legend.

INC: Let's step back from the human element of the business for a second. How about the numbers? What financial information do you track that helps you run the business?

RODDICK: Well, for starters, I don't want to know all those financial breakdowns. The business has financial controls that my husband, Gordon and the financial folks monitor. I'm interested in only three statistics—gross and product sales, store traffic and average sale per customer. If any of those start veering downwards, I'll start asking questions about customer care, displaying of products, price, that kind of thing.

If the average sale goes down, my concern would be that the staff is getting bored. It would mean that my staff is not talking to customers enough. They're just being there like cash and wrap.

INC: Can you give us your definition of business?

RODDICK: It sure isn't the traditional definition. Traditional business has been controlled by the science of business. The science of business is very theoretical. It is the computer output of figures. Good business has been esteemed to be solely the playing area of money. Therefore, it becomes a science—how to make more money.

Roddick's definition of business

If you say the business of business is to generate profits to create jobs, that takes on a different tone. Or the responsibility of business is to keep your employees breathless, that's definitely a whole new tone. It frees your thinking from just getting out profits and undervaluing the humanness of business.

I see business as a far more renaissance concept, where the human spirit comes into play, the environment where you work comes into play, and the aesthetics of the environment....it just takes on a slightly different vocabulary than just being stuck creating profits. That's deeply boring.

I believe quite passionately that there is a better way. I think we can rewrite the book on business. I think we can trade ethically; be committed to social responsibility, global responsibility; empower our employees without being afraid of them. It's showing that business can have a human face, and God help us if we don't try.

INC: Many of us grew up with the sense that business was divorced from every other aspect of our lives. We were never really given the information about what business really is. If one of your missions is to make people more responsible, you give them the information they need to be able to accomplish that.

RODDICK: I think so. I think there is the need for more information and a whole new vocabulary for business. The assumption, the myth, is that business is always the robber baron or get-rich-quick schemes. I don't see it like that. I actually see it as ennobling. It's been going on for centuries. It's trading, a simple activity centered on direct relationships between people. Very human. It's saying, "I love that. Can I buy it?" It's making your product so glorious that people don't mind buying it from you at a profit.

INC: If we met someone who had worked as a salesperson in one of your shops for a few years and had left, what is it that you would most want that person to say The Body Shop did for her?

RODDICK: That's lovely. Did for her. Valued her labor. Made her feel that she was powerful. That she had a role as a citizen. Created a sense of curiosity, not only about her own body and her well-being, but about the environment and the world around her. Created a habit of care, because it is a habit with the young, you have to force them to care. And the last thing I would have hoped we had done, which is toughest of all, is to convince her that this is no dress rehearsal: You've got one life and so just lead it. And try to be remarkable. Try to be remarkable.

EPILOGUE

As of mid-1992, The Body Shop continues to expand at a record pace. A Body Shop branch opens every three days worldwide, with stores now totaling over 700 in 41 countries, excluding the United Kingdom with its 200-plus stores. The fastest-growth market is now the United States, having, at last count, 78 stores. The Body Shop management maintains that none of the markets in which they operate has yet reached saturation point.

The company's growth has not changed its basic philosophy, believing profits and principles go hand-in-hand. To date, The Body Shop has 475 community projects worldwide, and sources its products in Third World countries ranging from Nepal to Bangladesh to the Amazon Basin. A major campaign for the company over the past two years has been the Romania Relief Appeal, which supplies funds and labor to upgrade Romania's notorious orphanages.

Roddick maintains a harrowing schedule sourcing products and visiting stores worldwide. In order to communicate and motivate from a distance, a video crew follows her on her travels, producing shows that are sent weekly to all the shops around the world. As part of efforts to encourage commitment and empowerment, in July 1991, The Body Shop launched its Partnership Scheme—allowing the staff of selected company-owned stores to become part-owners of their shops.

Interest in The Body Shop, its principles, and its success continues to grow, now fueled by Roddick's best-selling book, *Body and Soul*, which hit the bookstores in September 1991.

4

ONE OF THE FASTEST-GROWING COMPANIES
IN HISTORY WAS ALSO THE MOST REVOLUTIONARY
IN PEOPLE MANAGEMENT—ALL OF THE
EMPLOYEES WERE OWNERS, MANAGERS AND
JACK-OF-ALL-TRADES.

DON BURR

Editor-in-Chief George Gendron conducted this interview with the founder of People Express Airlines at company headquarters in Newark, N.J. in June 1985 and it appeared in *Inc.*'s August 1985 issue.

We all have to choose, someone once said, between perfection of life and perfection of work. At People Express Airline Inc., the founding father wants both—for everybody.

Of all the legends of recent American entrepreneurship, Donald Burr's is one of the most astonishing. In four years, he has built an airline, the ninth largest in the United States, which last spring reached the $1-billion mark in annualized revenues. Starting with 250 employees, the airline now has about 4,000. Starting with 3 used Boeing 737s, the airline now has 22 737s, 45 727s, and four 747s, which carry a million passengers a month to 39 cities in America and to one abroad, London. Starting with a verminous, empty terminal in Newark, N.J., the carrier now boasts a facility that, if not the most elegant in the industry, is certainly the most colorful, teeming with mobile Americans of every description, all eager to take advantage of Donald Burr's realization of a great idea: the discount airline.

Growth like that would be dizzying in Silicon Valley; in the transportation industry, it approaches the miraculous. Yet even so, the legend of Donald Burr only begins with growth. The rest of it, fittingly, is about people, and the transformation Burr is trying to bring about in the way people work together. It is an approach to human resources that enshrines self-management and voluntary cooperation. At People Express, every effort is made to eradicate or suppress the two most sacrosanct characteristics of organized work: hierarchy and specialization. There is no working class at People Express, no executive class. Everyone is a manager, and everyone (even the pilots, who are called "flight managers") does a regularly scheduled turn at everyone else's work. With this policy, called "cross utilization," Burr seems to be trying to reinstate the ancient ideal of the well-rounded man.

With the company's stock-participation policy—every employee is required to purchase some stock, if necessary with a no-interest loan from the company itself— he seems to be trying to realize the equally ancient ideal of a commonwealth, in which each member acquires the pride and energy of an owner. Thirty-three percent of the airline is employee-owned, and the rags-to-riches stories that its success has made possible among the employees are all part of Burr's legend.

Burr denies that he is conducting a "social experiment" at People Express. "It's a hard-driving, capitalist business," he says to everyone, celebrant and skeptic alike. "You don't just want to make a buck. You want people to become better people."

The skeptics have become more numerous recently—in the media, on Wall Street, and even within the great people-centered undertaking of People Express itself. Doubts seem to have been triggered by the late 1984-early 1985 operating losses, followed by a plunge in the company's stock price from a high of 25 to below 10. The set-back stemmed in large part from an inevitable ratcheting-up of the competition, as the more traditional airlines learned to slash prices almost as well as People Express.

INC.: People Express has had a couple of pretty tough innings on Wall Street recently, which must have had an enormous impact on morale. Does that concern you?
BURR: It kills me. I want people to love this place. It drives me nuts walking around seeing people unhappy. But there are several clear reasons for it. For two

quarters in a row now—the last of 1984 and the first of 1985—we've lost money, and in the last quarter we didn't pay any profit sharing. When we lost money and didn't pay profit sharing, it broke the mystique.

INC.: Mystique?
BURR: People Express has a mystique; we couldn't do anything wrong. We just bought planes, hired people, and put them in the air. Grow, grow, grow. The expectations at this place are colossal. And self-generated. The good old guys, the well-managed old companies, had spent the time to learn how to compete with us better. They were competing with us better. So we had to adapt our tactics and strategy. But any time you introduce large-scale change, it causes morale problems. You have to explain it all to everybody, and a lot of people don't get it right away. So I have to tell them again, and again, and again. It causes disruption, anxiety, uncertainty.

> **Introducing large-scale change**

INC.: How do you combat that?
BURR: You try to share the vision with them. But it's really hard to articulate the vision so that people will get with it. There's a constant, constant battle over the question, "Are you doing enough for me? I don't think you are, so we're getting a union." I'm sure it's everywhere, but you'd think you'd be able to set an objective and a structure clear enough so that people generally would be able to accept it and not do so much carping. It's frustrating to see large numbers of people not get it. I suppose our expectations are much too high.

INC.: You've been talking about people not "getting it." What is it exactly that you want them to understand?
BURR: The six precepts, the goals of People Express—those six items that we live by. The first one, of course, is service, growth, and development of people. The second one is to be the best provider of transportation for people. The third is to develop the best leadership. The fourth is to be a role model. The fifth is simplicity; and the sixth is to maximize profits. Those are the things we teach everybody here. That is our objective. If people ask, "Where are we going, where are we headed?" that's it.

Why can't you teach this? What is it that prevents people from seeing these things? Why wouldn't you want to see these precepts? They're absolutely gorgeous. They're pristine in their beauty and clarity. But I've got a lot of pilots around here that call them Kool-Aid. "Have you had your Kool-Aid today?" There are guys who absolutely resist the notion.

INC.: But isn't this just growing pains? You've gone from 250 to 4,000 employees, after all, in four years.

BURR: You start out with a set of ideals. Really lofty ideals. You believe that things ought to be done this way, and you get a bunch of people together who say, "Yeah, right on, let's create this great environment where people are going to live together and we'll all work together and we'll make a great family." And you start out

CEO reflects on the sour effects of growth

with 10 people and then go to 15. They see it. They might not be able to articulate it the way you can, but they're coming along, and over the months and years, they're getting able to say it in pretty nice ways and even add some nuances. But now you hire 100 people, and then you hire another 100, and another 100, and now you get a lot of people saying, "What is this Kool-Aid stuff?"

Actually, it's the antithesis of Kool-Aid. You have two parameters at People Express: Take care of people; take care of customers. How could you be more free? I tell everyone, "Make all the mistakes you want, fly the planes upside down. No problem. But just remember, we're always guided by those precepts. We take care of each other. And we take care of customers. Within those bounds, you can do just about anything."

But then you get people coming around saying, "I don't like you. I don't like this place. I'm going to get into a union, and we're going to force you to pay us more to work less." So the water drip starts, and your heart and your soul listen, and you wonder what you've done to deserve this. Here we've provided people with 8 million shares of stock, 100% medical/dental, profit sharing. . . . We've done everything we could to provide people with this environment to have some fun and do well. And they don't like it, I guess. So this garbage starts to seep into your brain, and you say, "What the hell did I do that I shouldn't have done? Where did I go wrong? Why is it people can't see?"

INC.: Maybe your vision for the company, your expectations, will always exceed people's abilities to live up to them.
BURR: Well, I think that's a real problem for leaders. I think an issue of our times is how we develop new leadership and keep it going. How do we support good leadership? We talk about supporting our people here at People Express. Coaching and helping and teaching all of the people who are doing work of various kinds. But we don't talk much at all, anywhere, about how we support good leaders. In fact, across the whole of American society, there's a sort of back pressure that leaders are somehow to be distrusted. It's kind of like entrepreneurs 20 years ago. Entrepreneurs 20 years ago were promoters. Dirty capitalistic promoters. Today, all of a sudden, entrepreneur is a golden word.

INC.: Well, what could make you happier? For instance, do you have any plans to expand?
BURR: We need to be able to take on other entities, either develop them ourselves or acquire them, anything from Twin Otters, say, to a TWA. Physically, financially, we could be out there bidding for a TWA today. But the human-resource strategy won't allow it as of today.

INC.: What do you mean?
BURR: We have not yet proven out our concepts of behavior in an airline setting. Not so we're confident enough to be able to replicate them in another setting. We haven't yet proven to ourselves that they work at People Express consistently. We have not proven that the unique productivity of People Express is based on our people systems. My financial officer, Bob McAdoo, sits there and says, "Yeah, Don, give me a break. If we didn't do all those other things that you had us do in terms of the equipment and the seats and the rest of it, all that people stuff wouldn't be worth anything." There's a kernel of truth to that. But I really believe that we would never have been able to grow to a billion dollars in annualized revenues in just under four years without our particular type of organization. If we had not put in the flat structure and the free environment, we never would have made it.

INC.: There are people who say that you are so lost in your vision of what the company can be, in human terms, that you forget what it must be as a business.

BURR: On the contrary, I happen to think that the vision is directly transmitted to the customer. To the extent we can get everybody on board knowing where we're headed and why, and to the extent that they buy it, to that extent they're going to be better motivated and better able to cope with the customer demands out there. It doesn't mean we don't have to go around doing a lot of things like sweeping the ramp and keeping the planes clean. Specific operational problems. But the specific operational problems get done relatively better by people who know what they're doing and why they're doing it than they do by people who don't.

INC.: Perhaps the problem with your human-resource approach is that the real dividends, the business dividends are more long-term than short-term. I'm not sure your people have been around long enough for the company to really begin to experience the benefits of your approach to human resources.

BURR: I couldn't agree with you more. I think you're absolutely right on the money. Wall Street, of course, wants you to produce it all two or three years ago. Wall Street is very impatient. I've told them over and over again, you've got to wait. We can't create a billion-dollar company in four years and make a hundred million dollars in the process. It doesn't happen that way.

INC.: Your equity-participation policy must have created problems for you; all those employees whose stock has been taking a beating lately.

Equity-participation policy

BURR: I get remarkably little back pressure on the stock. I warned everybody who came to People Express about the stock when they walked in. Every single class that I've taught, I've said, "Hey, this stuff goes up and it goes down. So be happy when it's up, because you're going to be miserable when it's down. That's the nature of stock." But are our people happy about it? No. Obviously they're unhappy about it, but I don't think it's that big a deal. Now we're all waiting for it to go back up again.

INC.: One of the fundamental components of your human-resource approach is job rotation. Do you still have a high commitment to it?
BURR: Yes. The worst problems with the job rotation came early on. The problem was just getting enough people trained to be able to do everything. There were constant complaints that we didn't have consistent behavior, consistent performance. Checking people in properly, doing the right things on the planes. Everywhere you looked, people were moaning and dying over inconsistent performance.

Adjusting to job rotation

Everybody was saying, "This will never work. We're telling you, Don, we've got to have the same person at the same job every day." We said, "Bear with us, it will work." And now you don't hear that anymore. What we're trying to do is to get a better fit between what the group wants, what each individual wants to do, and what he or she can do.

INC.: What is it you are looking for in an employee?
BURR: We look for all the ordinary things that everybody else looks for. I guess the one area where I think we've had some success is in looking for service-oriented people, people who are a little more likely than the average person to go out of their way to help you out. The test we use screens them, not for that quality, but against its obverse, which is your antisocial, negative, cynical, downbeat character. That type of person isn't normally prone to be overly helpful to other people.

INC.: Do you ever think that maybe you're faced with a difficult choice here? You want the company to slow down, consolidate. But are you the best person to oversee that process? You seem to get excited only when talking about the future. On the other hand, if you leave . . . well, the human-resource policy is your vision, and without you to sustain it, how long will it last?
BURR: Well, I never thought of it quite that way. That's a nice formulation. I'm reasonably well convinced that the place really does need to take a breather. But I hadn't thought that I might not be interested in sitting around nursemaiding it. That had not occurred to me. But I'm the one who slowed it down, not the board,

not Wall Street. I'm the one who said, "Hey, look, let's sell a couple planes, let's slow down and tidy the place up a little bit." That's my direction, and I'm doing it because I really believe it needs to be slowed down.

INC.: One of the things that strikes me, just walking around this place, is how tangible the signs of your accomplishments are. I mean, you just look out your window, and there they are, every day, big planes that are dramatic, physical reminders of what you guys have been able to accomplish. Doesn't it give you an extraordinary sense of achievement, a thrill?
BURR: You know, it used to. When the first planes were delivered here, three whole planes, now that was a thrill. Watching the first People Express flight ever take off; that was something. Now when I look out there, I don't know, there are just so damn many planes out there. It's just not the same anymore.

EPILOGUE

To quote Burr, "any powerful system is bound to have its own pathologies," and People Express was no exception. Within a year after this interview was conducted, People Express was sold to Continental Airlines, which also absorbed its $700-million debt burden. According to Burr, arrogance played a major role in the airline's demise. Its rapid success led to overconfidence and contentment, a state of mind that allowed the company to take its eye off the ball. Where People Express was particularly vulnerable was the area of information technology, or the airline reservation system. Just a couple of airlines soon monopolized the entire reservation network, causing a good many smaller or weaker carriers to close shop.

The People Express "experiment" continues to be studied by academicians and CEOs alike, who examine the successes and failures of People's management policies. Burr contributes to the exercise by delivering speeches on the subject, and is currently at work on a book that reevaluates the experience and tells the tale of a five-year-old company whose revenues approached $2 billion before closing its doors.

Burr does not rule out the possibility of starting another airline and reviews every deal that comes his way. If he were to do it all over again, he would only slightly modify the principles of People Express. First, given the tremendous training requirements that have to exist for cross-utilization to work, Burr would be more strategic the next time about its introduction and execution rather than overburden the company and its people. Second, he would make a point to promote only from within. And third, he would guard against raising his own expectations and those of the employees so high that satisfaction remains out of reach. "Looking back," Burr ponders, "the company probably overcommitted to the individual at the expense of the company as a whole."

HARRY QUADRACCI

Editors George Gendron and Bo Burlingham conducted this
interview with the CEO of Quad/Graphics Inc. at his office in
Pewaukee, Wisc. in mid-1986 and it appeared in
Inc.'s December 1986 issue.

Harry V. Quadracci once described his fabulously successful and profitable
company as a "social experiment," and to an outsider, there seems to be some
truth to it. For in the course of taking Quad/Graphics Inc. from less than
$1 million to more than $300 million over the past 15 years, Quadracci has broken
most of the rules.

Early on, for example, he put his employees on a three-day, 36-hour workweek,
which made it easier for the company to keep its presses running round the clock
and sent productivity shooting up 20%. Later, he launched Camp Quad, where customers come to be educated about the printing business, and bought a little red
schoolhouse for employee-training sessions. He shares ownership with employees—
they now control more than 40% of the company's stock—and lets them run new
divisions as entrepreneurial ventures. One of those divisions, Quad/Tech, develops
new printing technologies, which it then sells to other printers, including Quad's
competitors, contributing a significant portion to Quad/Graphics' profits.

Quadracci attributes much of his company's success to "thinking small." But that
has not stopped him from signing up some of the biggest names in the magazine

industry—including *Newsweek*, *U.S. News & World Report*, and *Time*—as customers.

INC.: There's been a good deal written about your company over the years—the aggressive research-and-development effort, the education center for employees and customers, the three-day workweek, and so forth. But readers out there who run small companies say to themselves, "That's nice, but I can't afford that. My business isn't large enough. I'm still worrying about survival."

> Getting things done by thinking small

QUADRACCI: You know, whether it's R&D or employee training or customer service, it's always easy to say you'll do that when you have the money. But the truth is that if you don't do it at the beginning, you'll never do it. There's nothing we do now at Quad/Graphics that we didn't do during our first five years. In most cases, anybody can do these things—it's just a matter of thinking small, of starting in some small way—of doing *something*.

INC.: I think it was your annual report that said you're almost running a technology company more than a manufacturing company now.

QUADRACCI: We're a know-how company, a knowledge company, an R&D company—because where else are the ideas going to come from? And that's why we have to spend so much time on training and education. Because unlike some high-tech company out in Silicon Valley or something, we don't hire a lot of engineers. The average employee who joins my company looks like a loser.

INC.: Loser?

QUADRACCI: They are the kids in the class who didn't go to college, who didn't make it in school for some reason, and in many ways have nowhere to go. And what we do is to get them to elevate their sights, to become something more than they had ever hoped to be. I like to say that we get extraordinary results from ordinary people. Instead of thinking of themselves as printers, we get them to think of themselves as trained technicians who run the computers that run the press. And we can do that because so much of the drudge work has been eliminated from their jobs. Now, they have jobs that they can be proud of, which, in terms of improved quality, is perhaps the most important thing of all. Because by using technology to make ours a better, happier, more satisfying place to work, employees take more pride in what they do. And the quality of what is produced is improved even beyond what the technology can do directly.

> **Using technology and training to build self-esteem**

INC.: All of which must require a good deal of training on your part.

QUADRACCI: You can't have a technology company without also being a training company. And this is something we've understood right from the beginning. We like to think that we have an enlightened management philosophy. But enlightened management works best on enlightened employees. They're not born that way—they have to be indoctrinated. You don't have time to argue with them. Our attitude is, You're 18 years old. You're coming to work for Quad/Graphics. Yours is not to reason why. Welcome to boot camp. For the next three years, you're going to learn our way—and it's your responsibility to learn. We're going to give you the proper equipment, and it's your responsibility to educate yourself to use it.

INC.: What exactly does that mean?

QUADRACCI: We keep the training where it belongs, with the individual managers—all managers are responsible for training their own crews. In addition, we have an education department with a staff of 18, and a little red schoolhouse where we have courses all the time ranging from remedial reading and math to technical computer programming. And so on Monday, Tuesday, and Wednesday, employees will run the presses, and then on Friday mornings, they go to school. It's a tremendous staff-development system—the kids really take off.

INC.: That raises the same problem we asked about before. All this education stuff is great if you can afford a little red schoolhouse and can afford to have your employees set aside one day a week for courses. But how does somebody running a small shop do something like that?

> **The cost of training the workforce**

QUADRACCI: Who says it has to cost a lot of money? Forget

the schoolhouse. Forget the staff. When we started, we did training on a strictly voluntary basis. And, in fact, it is still done on a voluntary basis.

INC.: Your people don't get paid for training time?
QUADRACCI: No—that's on their free time. Nor do they get promotions based on going to school—although they often learn something that will make them promotable. Even the instructors come in on a voluntary basis. And they love it. Nobody wants to run a press anymore—they all want to teach!

INC.: We also hear they like to teach customers . . .
QUADRACCI: Camp Quad, our sleep-away printing camp.

INC.: Where did that idea come from?
QUADRACCI: Well, when the company first got started, if customers came to watch a job or approve the color or whatever, there really weren't enough of us in the office to escort them around. The escort is sort of traditional in the business—I don't know whether the escort is to protect the customer from the employee or the employee from the customer. But in our case, it didn't matter, because there was no other way to do it except to let the customer rub elbows with the press operators. And we found out early on that many of these customers really didn't know much about printing at all—they were just faking it.

INC.: Faking it?
QUADRACCI: Yeah. You'd get these guys in their fifties who'd been in charge of buying printing all their lives, and they didn't know what they were doing. They'd always bluffed it—and nobody had ever called their bluffs, so they never learned. So we let them observe the process and let them know as much as possible about what was going on. And after a while, the manufacturing director of a magazine would say, "Jeez, my art director should know about this," or "My sales department should know about this."

And so eventually we decided to formalize that by offering some training seminars at a campground nearby, which we call Camp Quad. We do it about eight times a year, back to back, about 35 people at a crack.

INC.: Just to play the devil's advocate here—why go to the trouble and expense of educating customers who will ask more questions and be more demanding? Why not just let them keep on bluffing?

QUADRACCI: Because I want them to print the best magazines at the lowest possible cost, so that they can sell more magazines and more ad pages and we can get more printing. Remember, our customer is really our customers' customer. And frankly, the camp also helps us develop a really harmonious partnership with the customer that makes it easier to deliver a good product and gives us an edge in developing new products that publishers might use.

INC.: Just to get a sense of it, what is your R&D budget, say, for this year?

QUADRACCI: We don't have budgets.

INC.: You don't have budgets?

QUADRACCI: Why should we? You know, for some reason or another, the whole aspect of the information explosion and computers has reached a blind spot when it comes to the accounting group. Why is it that so many companies insist on having a 12-month budget, drawn up in November of one year, based on still-incomplete numbers, that will be the bible for running the company as far away as December of the following year? Why do that when we have a computer now that can give me a profit-and-loss statement today on what we did on a press yesterday? Isn't actual performance a better guide—a better budget—than a budget?

> **A company with no budgets**

INC.: One reason for a budget, perhaps, is to anticipate what capital needs you'll have. In your annual report, you boast that you've just placed one of the biggest orders in printing history—$50 million worth of equipment. How do you anticipate capital for something like that with no budget?

QUADRACCI: We have a simple rule: if you can finance it, buy it. That's what it comes down to—ready, fire, aim. We go out and order 14 presses that will be ready in two years, roughly. And then, based on some inquiries and sales calls and my gut feeling about our ability to sell, we may locate two of them in Saratoga Springs,

N.Y., maybe another two in Lomira, Wis. But there is no way that you can plan that—it's more heart than head. It's hunchmanship.

INC.: What's the difference between a hunch and a guess?
QUADRACCI: A hunch is something you have after you go out and talk to your customers, to see what they're feeling—what they did this year, what they think for 1987. It's taking the temperature of the customers almost daily. And if you're an owner, you've got to be there, you've got to sense it for yourself. There is no substitute for hands on.

That's the problem with a large company. In a large company, managers rely on reports, but you cannot feel reports. You've got to be there—in the field, in the plant, out in the street. You don't learn the business from salespeople or budget planners. You learn the business from the clients—who, by the way, love to teach. And on that basis, you're ready to make hunches.

INC.: And doesn't that approach to long-range decision-making—buy it if you can finance it, go on your hunches—lead to rather large mistakes?
QUADRACCI: Look, the reason you have a bad-debt reserve is because if you are aggressive in your sales, you're going to have some people who don't pay. The same goes for hunchmanship and planning—you've got to make allowances for mistakes.

In the technology area, for example, if you don't have what I like to call "perfect failures," then you're not being aggressive enough in your R&D. And the larger you get, the bigger the perfect failures you can afford. We had great success putting two guys in a basement of a summer house—and as a result we started Quad/Tech, which develops new printing technologies that we then sell to other printers. We had a perfect failure when we developed a $780,000 folding machine that didn't work. Three guys worked two years because we felt sure there had to be a better way to deliver a folded page. And when it became apparent finally that it wasn't going to work, they felt terrible about it. But why should they have? By making that mistake, they explored the alternative.

INC.: Trial and error. Start early. Think small. These are your refrains.
QUADRACCI: Look, we are living in an age of change—change that we no longer

measure in evolutionary terms. If you're going to succeed in business today, you have to thrive on change, think in terms of change, assume that whatever is here today is going to be different tomorrow. You have to eat change for breakfast—that's what I tell new employees. And that's the spirit that goes all the way back here—before we were big, before we were very profitable, before there was a little red schoolhouse or Quad/Tech or Camp Quad. The trick was to keep telling ourselves, "There must be a better way." And most of the time, there has been.

EPILOGUE

As Quadracci is wont to say, he "eats change for breakfast." No longer. Now Quadracci is proud to say, he and everyone at Quad/Graphics "eats change for breakfast, lunch, and dinner." It would seem that this philosophy continues to pay off for the company. In the six years since this interview was conducted, Quad/Graphics's sales have increased 35% each year on average, and employees have gone from 2,100 in 1986 to over 5,300 in 1992.

But more noteworthy than the company's continued success despite rough times in the publishing industry, have been the innovative ventures Quad has established internally for its employees. One start-up that has received a good deal of attention is the Quad/Wellness Network. For $2.50 a week, each employee is a member of the Network, which offers a job-site Fitness Center, personal trainers, diet counseling, sports facilities—everything to promote good health and preventive medicine. But, for that $2.50, each employee also gets total medical care at the Quad/Med Clinic and Pharmacy. The clinic serves the employees with nine on-site physicians, X-rays, a full-service lab, a minor surgery room, and rehabilitation facilities. Employee participation in the Network runs as high as 70% in some plants.

Since Quad prides itself on being a first-class service company, it believes it can provide better services to employees than going outside. Employee ventures include: Quad/Care (daycare for employee children, a state-certified kindergarten and after-school programs for older kids); Quad/Travel (travel agency); Quad/Cuisine (cafeteria company); Quad/Construction; and of course, Quad/Education with its 135 volunteer instructors.

TO SAVE SAS, CARLZON KNEW HE HAD TO
CHANGE ITS CULTURE. HE HAD TO REMOVE
THE FEAR AND ALLOW MISTAKES IN ORDER
TO INSPIRE SUCCESS.

JAN CARLZON

Editors George Gendron and Steve Solomon met the CEO of
Scandinavian Airlines System at his New York office in January of
1989. This interview appeared in *Inc.*'s May 1989 issue.

Scandinavian Airlines System (SAS) was flying into a headwind when Jan
Carlzon took command of it in 1981. The company was in the midst of com-
piling a loss of $20 million, its second straight losing year. Morale was low.
Employees were being laid off. Service was being slashed. The market for passenger
and freight services was stagnant. Carlzon immediately set out to make SAS "the
best airline in the world for the frequent business traveler." Toward that end, he
invested $45 million to upgrade every detail of service for the business traveler,
while cutting nearly as much from programs directed at tourists.

The most important change, though, came in the way he treated SAS employees.
To be market driven, he believed, the company had to be successful in its 50,000
"moments of truth" every day—those brief moments that occur whenever an SAS
employee delivers a service to one of its customers. That meant turning the organi-
zational chart upside down. No longer were middle managers to spend their time
making sure instructions were followed. Now, they were to support the frontline
people who have direct contact with customers, enabling them to make decisions

and solve problems on the spot.

And the results? SAS returned to profitability the year after Carlzon took over.

INC.: You don't seem to fit the image of the modern airline president.

CARLZON: I agree. I think there's an expectation that the president of an organization such as mine should be tough, ruthless, driving people to do their best. Of course, I think my way gets people to really do their best.

INC.: How's that?

CARLZON: In my experience, there are two great motivators in life. One is fear. The other is love. You can manage an organization by fear, but if you do you will ensure that people don't perform up to their real capabilities. A person who is afraid doesn't dare perform to the limits of his or her capabilities.

INC.: Why not?

CARLZON: Because people are not willing to take risks when they feel afraid or threatened. But if you manage people by love—that is, if you show them respect and trust—they start to perform up to their real capabilities. Because, in that kind of atmosphere, they dare to take risks. They can even make mistakes. Nothing can hurt.

> ◀ **Taking risks and allowing mistakes**

INC.: Now wait a minute. Those are wonderful sentiments, but we're talking about running a business here. What do you mean, employees "dare to take risks"? Are you sure you want them to?

CARLZON: Absolutely. Let me give you an example from my own company. It's a story about a flight that was delayed because of heavy snowfall in Stockholm. Normally, we sell coffee, cookies, and sandwiches on domestic flights. But because of the delay and the weather, the purser on this flight decided to give the snacks away. Since they would be free, she figured she'd need enough for 80% to 90% of the passengers. So she called SAS Service Partner, our catering company, and asked for that amount. But the man in charge said she couldn't have it because it was out of our routine. She said she'd take responsibility. He still refused.

What could she do? Well, she realized that Finnair, which is one of our competitors, is also a strong customer of Service Partner. So she took the cash she had and went to the purser on the Finnair flight standing next to hers and asked him to order 60 coffees and cookies. She said, "I will pay for it if you can put it on the Finnair account." So he called Service Partner, and the man there couldn't refuse because Finnair is an extraordinary customer. The snacks were delivered, and she carried them in her hands to the SAS flight. To me, this is an extremely good example of a person daring to grab responsibility.

INC.: OK, but let's be realistic. That sort of individual initiative can go too far. Employees can just as easily spend too much money rectifying a problem or give away what they shouldn't.
CARLZON: Yes, I suppose that has happened, but such mistakes aren't important. What's the danger of giving away too much? Are you worried about having an oversatisfied customer? That's not much of a worry. You can forget about an oversatisfied customer, but an unsatisfied customer is one of the most expensive problems you can have.

INC.: How do you mean?
CARLZON: To get a satisfied customer back is just about free. To get new customers has a price, but to keep satisfied customers is almost without cost. On the other hand, it costs a small fortune to get dissatisfied customers back. So the danger is not that employees will give away too much. It's that they won't give away anything because they don't dare.

INC.: So you aren't worried that your people will make mistakes.
CARLZON: On the contrary, I want them to make mistakes. I heard once about a company president who told his people, "I want you to make at least two mistakes a week." What was he really saying? "I know you're so good that—to make 2 wrong decisions a week—you must be able to make 20 to 30 right ones. I want you to make decisions." The same goes for me. The dangerous thing is to not make decisions.

INC.: This all seems a little soft. What if you can't afford these mistakes? What if you're not making money?

CARLZON: We *weren't* making money at SAS when I came here. We were in a desperate situation, and that's the worst time to focus on preventing mistakes and controlling costs. First, we had to increase revenues. We had to decide what business we were going to do and go to work on the revenue side. Then we could think about cutting costs, because only then would we know which costs could be cut without losing competitiveness.

INC.: Can we go back to a comment you made a moment ago? You said, "First, we had to decide what business to do and go to work on the revenue side." What did you mean by that?

CARLZON: I mean that, before you can start managing effectively, you must know who is your customer and what is your product. The most important advice I ever got in business came from a colleague of mine who was quite a character. One day he kicked me and said, "Never forget, Jan, that the most difficult thing in doing good business is to say no to bad business, the bad opportunities." He meant that you must always decide who your customer is, and what product you are going to present to your specific customer. And you should say no to every option that is not related to that customer's need, or to that production, or to that performance. You should say no even if the option could be profitable in its own right.

> **Defining what business you're in**

We said we want to be the preferred airline for the frequent business traveler, and we are not allowed to invest one penny or spend one resource in any activity not related to the business market. We went through the entire company asking ourselves, "Is this service, is this production, is this person related to the business traveler's needs or not?" If the answer is yes, we have to ask ourselves if we have enough or too much of that resource, and should we increase or decrease it. If the answer is no, we have to get rid of it immediately. Because it's more important to be 1% better in the right detail than to be 100% better in the wrong detail.

INC.: That's probably one area in which large companies differ dramatically

from small companies—getting people to focus on the small details.

CARLZON: I don't know. If you have five employees, you see them every day, and you can communicate with them directly. If you have 34,000 employees, you have a tremendous resource and a fantastic challenge. You have to give very clear objectives in a large organization. But the basic management approach is the same. In both cases, you still need to show people respect and faith.

INC.: But doesn't a company get to a size at which it becomes unwieldy—when you just can't get your message out to everybody anymore?

CARLZON: I don't think so. If you have a good message, you can get an entire nation to hear it. Good messages will be spread.

INC.: How do you spread them?

CARLZON: Show biz. It's all show biz.

INC.: What do you mean?

CARLZON: I produce the show. I think I am a strategic person. But how do I get people to grab the strategy, to get it under their skin, to get a feel for it, to get it? I can't write it in a manual. I must make a show of it. I motivate people through the show. Right? Communication. And it is not manipulating—it is a way of getting the message across.

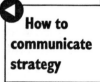

How to communicate strategy

INC.: Give us an example.

CARLZON: To some extent, I've used the media to get my message across to people. I know that, if I send out an internal memo, 10% of our people will read it, and 2% will remember it. But if there's an article about SAS in the newspaper, they will all read it, because they are interested in their company. I even published a book to get across the message—*Moments of Truth*. My main mission there was to reach people inside the company, because I knew they were going to read it.

INC.: Is that how you see your job, as the communicator of the strategy?

CARLZON: Yes, I suppose so. My job is not to make business; my job is to ensure that other people can make business.

INC.: OK, but you must have to keep your message fairly simple if you want to get it across on that scale.

CARLZON: Oh, definitely. I want to keep it simple. I say, "We want to be the preferred airline for the frequent business traveler." It can't be misunderstood. If you start to give goals that can be misunderstood, you have to begin again.

INC.: Don't you worry that such a goal leaves too much room for interpretation?

CARLZON: Well, you must provide a framework in which people can act. For example, we have said that our first priority is safety, second is punctuality, and third is other services. So, if you risk flight safety by leaving on time, you have acted outside the framework of your authority. The same is true if you don't leave on time because you are missing two catering boxes of meat. That's what I mean by a framework. You give people a framework, and within the framework you let people act.

INC.: You're talking about communicating strategy, but you also had to communicate a different way of running a business when you came to SAS, didn't you? How did you convince managers, for example, to adopt your style of management?

CARLZON: I'm not sure I have convinced so many people. If they think I'm acting in a specific way, well, you know and I know that every manager wants to copy the chief executive especially if the company is successful. If I wear a jacket and trousers, managers will do so. If I play golf, more people will play golf. And so forth. It is natural for people to copy me if my way is successful. If it is bad, I think they will find other ways.

INC.: What about employees? After all, you were coming into a company in which people felt mistakes could cost them their jobs. Now, you tell them that they shouldn't worry about mistakes—they should take responsibility and make decisions. How do you get them to feel secure enough to do that?

CARLZON: There are no simple tricks. Just live up to it. And listen. Sooner or later, you'll hear about someone who made a decision that you think was very good in terms of the company's strategy. When you do, make sure that you give the person many strokes, and do it as officially as possible, so other people will learn from it. A positive example is the best way to create the right atmosphere. Of course, if you think someone made a wrong decision, let him know it, but tell him when you are alone—and don't let him view it as a punishment. Really, there are so many things you can do to give people the security to take responsibility. Over time, you do it by measuring and rewarding performance.

INC.: Not by show biz?
CARLZON: For a year or two, you can motivate people through emotion and show biz. They are hyped up for a while. But, for the long run, people must know they will be measured in an accurate way in relation to the responsibility they have been given. That's a good way of spreading security among people, and it's one area I didn't always understand as well as I do today.

INC.: Well, that raises another question—namely, how do you learn about this stuff, anyway? Did you always have this approach to management?

Learning how to manage

CARLZON: No, not at all. In fact, I started out just the opposite. I'd been appointed president of a company where I'd worked for six years with a team of managers about my age, which was 32 at the time. Although I would have been very disappointed if I hadn't been made president, I still got nervous about the attitude of the other managers. How would they look at me now? I felt that I had to show them I was the right man for the job. The company was in a bad situation, with big losses. I thought, "Now, I have to be the boss." I thought I had to prove I knew everything better than the others did—that I was quicker in analyzing things and making decisions and everything. So I started developing my ego, saying "I want this" and "I decide that."

INC.: What made you change?
CARLZON: I was lucky to have good friends around me. One of those good friends saw what was happening and came into my office. He said, "What the hell

are you doing? Do you think we chose you to be our boss because we wanted you to be somebody different from who you were? If you don't get back to being yourself, you will be a failure." This was a very good lesson to me. You see, I was insecure. He gave me one type of security by saying, "For heaven's sake, we respect you as you are, and we accept you as a boss because of who you are." The next thing, of course, was that we succeeded. I saw I could do things that people expected me to do, and that were good for the company. People liked me as boss. That gave me security and confidence.

INC.: In a sense, you're talking about mental health, aren't you? You're talking about how you feel about yourself. What your friend did was give you permission to be yourself, and that's a big part of leadership.
CARLZON: I can tell you, there are days when I feel very bad and I shouldn't leave my office. I should just stay at my desk. But when I feel fine, strong, I shouldn't stay a minute in my office. I should walk around and see my people, because just to walk around and dare to be strong, dare to give, is much more valuable than any decision I could make or any report I could read. What I give away then is mental health to the organization. You see what I mean? Isn't it right? It is right!

INC.: Do you actually put aside the reports and call it a day?
CARLZON: Sure. The most unproductive time we have is when we sit at our desks. Because the only thing we do is read history: what has already happened, what we cannot do anything about. Statistics, memorandums, reports, minutes of meetings. Then we have eight telephone calls to make, of which two are worthwhile. But when we leave our offices and start to walk around and talk to people, that's when we make things happen. You give your thoughts; you get thoughts back; you draw conclusions; perhaps you even make decisions.

INC.: What could make a day so bad you'd want to stay in your office?
CARLZON: Oh, various things. Ironically, some of our biggest problems have come from having too much success too fast.

INC.: What do you mean?

CARLZON: I mean that, after just two years, we were more profitable than we had ever been in history, and everyone was rating us the preferred airline for the business traveler. So we were there. As Arne Naess said when he climbed Mt. Everest, "I had a dream. I reached it. I lost the dream, and I miss it." It was the same for our whole organization. We had a dream, and we reached it, and we reached it very quickly.

INC.: What was so bad about that?
CARLZON: We didn't have another long-term objective. So people started to produce their own new objectives—not a common objective, but different objectives depending on where they were in the organization. You see, it had all been a little too easy. And we created frustration, because this is a psychological game. Do you know the song Peggy Lee sings, "Is That All There Is?"

INC.: Did you have that feeling?
CARLZON: Yes.

INC.: What did you do?
CARLZON: One thing I did was talk to Ingmar Bergman.

INC.: The director Ingmar Bergman?
CARLZON: Yes. Let me tell you a story about Bergman. I invited him to dinner one week before the premiere of "Hamlet" in Stockholm. He said, "You are crazy. It would be an insult to all your other guests. It would be like inviting me to dinner one week before my divorce. Do you know why? Because I start to build this play eight or nine months ago. First, I write the synopsis; then I select the artists. I involve them in my play, tell them what I expect from them, help them get the idea. We all work for the same objective: to make this play a fantastic play. But it is my play, my works, my scenery, my thoughts, my everything. So they rehearse, and I help them. I form them. And now—one week before the premiere—do you know what is happening? They've taken it over. They don't need me any more. I'm a spillover. Can you understand that? So don't invite me for dinner." OK, well, the

> **Having too much success too fast**

same thing goes for the president of a company.

INC.: What did you learn from that?
CARLZON: I learned that, before you reach an objective, you must be ready with a new one, and you must start to communicate it to the organization. But it is not the goal itself that is important.

INC.: What is important?
CARLZON: The fight to get there.

EPILOGUE

Carlzon believes that by getting out of his office, he passes on mental health to the company. In the past couple of years, Carlzon has rarely been found behind his desk. Events have overtaken the company, forcing tough reevaluations and painful decisions, with Carlzon out front giving information and rationalizing changes.

All airlines were hit hard by the Gulf War and the recession, and SAS was no exception. These events, coupled with changes in the EEC that are reminiscent of airline deregulation in the U.S., have all amounted to massive cost cuts in order for SAS to survive as a healthy airline leader in the years to come. The cost structures of European airlines are too high for any of the players to win a price war among themselves or against U.S. and Asian competitors. Subsequently, responsible airlines are reexamining their expenses, with SAS proceeding very strategically and with definitive productivity goals.

One goal, announced in January 1991, is to be 20% more productive by January 1993. It is estimated that attrition, relocation, and early retirement will account for half of the 3,500 jobs cut. The guiding light in cost-cutting decisions has been "to develop a company culture that eliminates all costs that the customers are not willing to pay for, a culture where it is unethical to carry costs that do not contribute to the success of the customers."

SAS so far is keeping pace with its goal benchmarks. Of the 38 unions, 35 have agreed to new contracts to date, leaving only the three pilot unions still at the negotiating table. Besides cost cuts in personnel, other parts of the productivity action plan include increased automation, product development, and new training programs for managers and customer service personnel.

At a recent SAS managers' conference, Carlzon restated his uneasiness with success and the state of mind it creates. He expressed that the changes being made now to respond to external pressures will only strengthen the company long term, stating "If we don't use a crisis, it's like standing on a platform and letting the train stop and depart without you. We must catch this train."